# THE FAITH

## OF THE

# CATHOLIC CHURCH

## A Summary

### Edited by
### Bishop David Konstant

*All booklets are published thanks to the
generous support of the members of the
Catholic Truth Society*

CATHOLIC TRUTH SOCIETY
PUBLISHERS TO THE HOLY SEE

"And this is eternal life, that they know you the only true God, and Jesus Christ whom you have sent" *(Jn 17:3)*.

"God, our Saviour, desires all to be saved and to come to the knowledge of the truth" *(1 Tim 2:3-4)*.

"There is no other name under heaven given among men by which we must be saved" *(Acts 4:12)*.

God, infinitely perfect and blessed in himself, in a plan of pure goodness freely created the human race to share his blessed life and is close to us at all times and in all places. God calls and helps each person, all human beings, to seek, know and love him with all their strength. Through his Son, whom he sent in the fullness of time as the Redeemer and Saviour, the Father gathers all people, scattered and divided by sin, into the unity of his family, the Church. Through Christ and in him, the Father invites them to become his adopted children in the Holy Spirit and so heirs to his blessed life. *(Catechism of the Catholic Church, n.1)*

# ❧ FOREWORD ❧

The *Catechism of the Catholic Church*, was solemnly promulgated by Pope John Paul II on 11 October 1992, to the Church and to all peoples. But because of its vast scope this rich doctrinal treasure is not immediately and easily accessible to everyone. This shorter version presents the contents of the *Catechism* more briefly, in question and answer form.

This *Summary* is for those who wish to gain a basic knowledge of the faith and moral teaching of the Catholic Church. Its purpose is to help clergy, teachers, catechists, enquirers and students (though it is not intended for children). The hope is that, by using this short book, many readers will be encouraged to explore the full text of the *Catechism* itself. Inevitably, an abbreviated version has not the balance and completeness of the full text, but it is hoped that this text will prove genuinely useful.

In using this *Summary* the reader should keep in mind that its purpose is "to help deepen understanding of faith", and that it is directed "towards the maturing of that faith, putting down roots in personal life, and shining forth in personal conduct" *(CCC, n. 24)*. In other words readers may use this text to help them discover and grow in faith. It is a tool for evangelisation and catechesis.

The order of treatment is that of the Catechism itself. It is faithful to its content, frequently quoting directly from it. In particular, a number of the *'In Brief'* sections from the full text have been used. There is also an analytical index. References to the *Catechism of the Catholic Church (CCC)* are given at the beginning of each of the four main parts.

I owe a large debt of gratitude to many people, and in particular to the author and publisher of the original work, to Andrew Summersgill who gave invaluable help with the translation, and to those who commented on the text and suggested improvements. I hope they are pleased with the final text.

✠ **David Konstant**

**Bishop of Leeds**

# Contents

**The Good Shepherd, early Christian period in marble. Museo Cristiano Lateranese, Rome, Italy.**

# PART ONE
## ❧ THE PROFESSION OF FAITH ❧

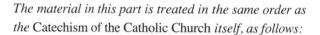

*The material in this part is treated in the same order as the* Catechism of the Catholic Church *itself, as follows:*

### THE PROFESSION OF FAITH: PART 1, §§ 26-1065

#### "I believe, we believe": Section 1, §§ 26-184

- Our openness to God: Chapter 1, §§ 27-49.
- God comes among us: Chapter 2, §§ 50-141.
- Our response: Chapter 3, §§ 142-184.

#### The Profession of Christian Faith: Section 2, §§ 185-1065

- God the Father: Chapter 1, §§ 185-421.
- Jesus Christ: Chapter 2, §§ 422-682.
- The Holy Spirit: Chapter 3, §§ 683-1065.

# — ❧ "I Believe, We Believe" ❧ —

## Our openness to God

### 1. How can we find true happiness?

By nature and by calling, we are religious beings. We
come from God and return to God. Everyone is created
to live in communion with him. Our hearts are restless
until they rest in him. Thus it is only with God that we
can find true and full happiness *(see nn. 226, 400)*.

### 2. Can we know God by reason?

By the light of reason we can come to know God and
to be certain that he exists.

### 3. How can we know and speak of God?

If we are to know God, we must listen to the message
of creation and to the voice of conscience. The infinite
variety of creation reflects God's infinite perfection and
helps us speak of God. However, the limitations of both
language and of our own understanding means that we
can never exhaust the mystery of his being: "If you
understood him, he would not be God" *(St Augustine)*.

## God comes among us

### 4. Has God spoken to mankind?

God has shown and given himself to us through love:
this is called Divine Revelation. God himself is the
complete response to all our questions about the
meaning and purpose of life.

### 5. When has God spoken to us?

God showed himself to our first parents, Adam and Eve, at the very beginning of time. After their fall into sin, he made a binding promise (his Covenant) that salvation would in time be found. Jesus Christ, the only Son of God, is the fullness of God's revelation of himself to us *(see nn. 39 ff.)*.

### 6. Where is divine revelation to be found?

Divine revelation is found in the Bible (called Sacred Scripture), and in Tradition.

### 7. What is Sacred Scripture?

Sacred Scripture consists of the writings of the Bible inspired by God. These are the 46 books of the Old Testament, and the 27 books of the New Testament.

### 8. Who is the author of Scripture?

There are many different human writers of Scripture who wrote under God's inspiration. But the one true author of Scripture is God himself. Thus we can be sure that these writings contain, without error, the truths of our salvation.

### 9. What is Apostolic Tradition?

Apostolic Tradition is the teaching given by Christ the Lord and by the Holy Spirit to the apostles that has come down to us in the Church.

## 10. Who can interpret the Bible and Tradition authoritatively?

The written or spoken word of God can be interpreted authoritatively only by the living teaching authority of the Church (the Magisterium), that is, by the Pope and by the bishops acting together with him *(see n. 205)*.

## OUR RESPONSE

## 11. How should we respond to God's call?

We should respond to God's call above all by an act of faith.

## 12. What is faith?

Faith is a gift from God which enables us to respond freely, through our intellect and will, to divine revelation. *(see n. 261)*

## 13. Is it necessary to believe in order to be saved?

Faith is necessary for salvation. As the Lord himself says: "Whoever believes and is baptised will be saved; whoever does not believe will be condemned" *(Mk 16:16)*.

## 14. Is there a brief expression of the truths we ought to believe?

There are various formulas of the truths of the faith. One such brief and ancient expression of faith is the "Symbol of the Apostles", or the Apostles' Creed:

I believe in God, the Father almighty,
creator of heaven and earth.
I believe in Jesus Christ, his only Son, our Lord.
He was conceived by the power of the Holy Spirit,
and born of the Virgin Mary.
He suffered under Pontius Pilate,
was crucified, died and was buried.
He descended to the dead.
On the third day he rose again.
He ascended into heaven,
and is seated at the right hand of the Father.
He will come again to judge the living
and the dead.
I believe in the Holy Spirit,
the holy Catholic Church,
the communion of saints.
the forgiveness of sins,
the resurrection of the body,
and the life everlasting. Amen.

# THE PROFESSION
## —— ❧ OF CHRISTIAN FAITH ❧ ——
### GOD THE FATHER

"I BELIEVE IN GOD, THE FATHER ALMIGHTY,
CREATOR OF HEAVEN AND EARTH"

**15. Who is God?**
God has revealed himself as I AM WHO I AM. His
very being is Truth and Love.

**16. What is the deepest mystery of our faith?**
The deepest mystery of our faith is the mystery of the
Blessed Trinity. In revealing this mystery of himself
as Father, Son and Holy Spirit, God teaches us
something about the nature of his being.

**17. How can we summarise this mystery?**
The Catholic faith consists in the veneration of the
one God in Trinity, and the Trinity in Unity, without
confusion of person or division of substance. There
are three distinct Persons in God: the Person of the
Father, the Person of the Son, and the Person of the
Holy Spirit. However the Godhead of the Father, the
Son and the Holy Spirit is one, equal in glory, and
co-eternal in majesty.

## 18. Do the three Persons have three distinct activities?

The divine Persons, inseparable in their substance, are also inseparable in what they do. But in the one divine operation the three Persons reveal their distinct role in the life of the Trinity, above all in the Incarnation of the Son, and the gift of the Holy Spirit.

## 19. What relationship do we have with the Blessed Trinity?

Through the grace of our Baptism "in the name of the Father and of the Son and of the Holy Spirit", we are given a share in the life of the Blessed Trinity. Here and now we live in the hiddenness of faith, and beyond death in eternal light *(see nn. 149, 150).*

## 20. What does it mean to say that God is omnipotent?

To say that God is omnipotent is to say that he is all-powerful. As scripture says, "nothing is impossible to God" *(Lk 1:37).*

## 21. Is it only the Father who is Creator?

The Father acts together with the Son and with the Holy Spirit. Although the work of creation is particularly attributed to the Father, all the Persons of the Trinity - Father, Son and Holy Spirit - are one and indivisibly the source of creation.

## 22. Was it necessary for God to have created the universe?

God created the universe freely, directly and without help.

## 23. What does "to create" mean?

To create means to produce and give being to that which has no being, that is, to call into existence out of nothing.

## 24. Why did God create the world?

God created the world to show and to communicate his glory, so that all creation might share in his truth, goodness and blessedness, and might give glory to him.

## 25. What is divine Providence?

Divine Providence is the way in which God, with wisdom and love, guides all creation to its final end.

## 26. Can we understand evil?

All evil, though deeply mysterious, has light thrown on it by Jesus Christ. Through his death and resurrection he conquered evil. We know through faith that God will not allow evil to triumph. "We know that in everything God works for good for those who love him" *(Rm 8:28).*

### 27. Is the visible universe all that exists?

Apart from the visible universe there is also an invisible world of angels and of human souls separated from the body by death.

### 28. Who are the angels?

The angels are spiritual creatures who unceasingly glorify God, and who work to carry out his saving plan for other creatures. They surround Christ, their Lord, and serve him especially in fulfilling his saving mission for all humankind.

### 29. What is a human being?

A human being is a unity of body and soul. Faith affirms that the soul is created directly by God, and is immortal.

### 30. In what condition did God create the first man and woman?

We know through revelation that the first man and woman were created by God in a state of holiness and justice (called 'original justice'). Their initial happiness in paradise, where there was no suffering and death, came from their intimate friendship with God; this gift was a share in the divine life.

**31. Did our first parents remain in this state of grace?**
Our first parents fell from this graced condition by sinning. This is known as the Fall.

**32. Who were the first creatures to sin?**
Some of the angels were the first creatures to sin. These fallen angels, of whom Satan or the Devil is the chief, are known as demons.

**33. What was the sin of the angels?**
The sin of Satan and the other angels was that they deliberately and freely refused to serve God. Their choice against God was final. They continue to tempt us to join them in their rebellion against God.

**34. What was the sin of our first parents?**
Tempted by the Evil One, at the beginning of history men and women abused their freedom, setting themselves up against God and wanting to go their own way apart from God.

**35. What were the results of this first sin?**
By his sin Adam, as the first man, lost the holiness and original justice which he had received from God.

**36. Does this first sin affect us all?**
Our first parents have passed to all their descendants a human nature wounded by their first sin, and hence

deprived of holiness and original justice. This deprivation is called 'original sin' *(see n. 150)*.

### 37. What are the effects of original sin?

As a result of original sin, human nature is weakened in its powers. It is subject to ignorance, suffering, the power of death and a tendency to sin. This inclination is called concupiscence *(see n. 229)*.

### 38. Is our situation hopeless?

Our situation is by no means hopeless. Christ's victory over sin has brought greater benefits than those lost through sin. "Where sin abounds, grace does more abound" *(Rm 5:20) (see n. 230)*.

### JESUS CHRIST

"I BELIEVE IN JESUS CHRIST, HIS ONLY SON, OUR LORD"

### 39. What does the name "Jesus" mean?

The name "Jesus" means "God who saves". The child born of the Virgin Mary is called "Jesus" because "he will save his people from their sins" *(Mt 1:21)*.

### 40. Why is Jesus called "Christ"?

The name "Christ" means "anointed", or "Messiah". Jesus is the Christ because God has consecrated him "with the Holy Spirit and with power" *(Ac 10:38)*. He is the one who was to come, the object of hope for the people of Israel *(cf. Ac 28:20)*.

### 41. Why is Jesus called "Son of God"?
The name "Son of God" shows the unique and eternal relationship of Jesus Christ to God his Father. He is the Only Begotten Son of the Father, and is himself truly God. To be a Christian one must believe that Jesus is the Son of God.

### 42. Why is Jesus called "Lord"?
The name "Lord" reveals the divine kingship. To confess or call on Jesus as Lord is to show faith in his divinity. "No one can say 'Jesus is Lord' except by the Holy Spirit" *(1 Co 12:3)*.

"JESUS CHRIST WAS CONCEIVED BY THE POWER OF THE HOLY SPIRIT AND BORN OF THE VIRGIN MARY"

### 43. What is the mystery of the Incarnation?
The Incarnation is the mystery of the wonderful union of the divine and human natures in the one Person of the eternal Son.

### 44. Why is Jesus unique?
Jesus is unique because he is the only Son of God the Father, from whom he became incarnate. He is the eternal Word and Image of the Father. At the time

chosen by God, he took on human nature, without losing the divine nature which he has from all eternity.

### 45. Is Jesus true God and true man?

Jesus Christ is true God and true man, in the unity of the divine Person. He is the one mediator between God and humankind.

### 46. Are the divine and human natures in Jesus intermingled?

The divine and human natures of Jesus Christ are not intermingled but are united in the one Person of the Son of God.

### 47. Does Jesus Christ have a human intellect and will?

Jesus Christ, being truly man, has a human intellect and will. These are perfectly harmonised and are subject to his divine intelligence and will, which he shares with the Father and the Holy Spirit.

### 48. Is Jesus like us in all things?

Jesus is like us in all things except sin.

### 49. Who is the Mother of Jesus?

The Mother of Jesus is the Blessed Virgin Mary. From among the children of Eve, God chose her to be the Mother of his Son. She is full of grace, and is the first and most exalted fruit of Redemption. She was preserved from every stain of original sin from the first moment of her conception, and remained free from all personal sin for the whole of her life.

## 50. Can we call Mary the Mother of God?

We can and must say that the Virgin Mary is "Mother of God", because she is the mother of the eternal Son of God made man, who is God himself.

## 51. Was Mary always a virgin?

Mary was always a virgin. She remained a virgin in conceiving her son, in giving birth to her son, and throughout her life. With her whole being she was "the handmaid of the Lord" *(Lk 1:38)*.

## 52. Who were the brothers of Jesus mentioned in the Gospel?

The brothers of Jesus mentioned in the Gospel were his close relatives. It was normal practice in those days to speak of cousins as brothers and sisters.

## 53. Did Mary have a part in the redemptive work of her Son?

Mary co-operated in the work of salvation freely and obediently. She uttered her "yes" in the name of the whole of humanity. By her obedience she became the new Eve, mother of all the living *(see n. 114)*.

## 54. Is Jesus' earthly life important for us now?

The whole of Jesus' life was one continual teaching: his silences, his miracles, his actions, his preaching, his prayer, his love for people, his special concern for children and for the poor, his acceptance of the complete sacrifice on the cross for the redemption of the world, and his resurrection from the dead, are the fulfilment of all God had promised and the completion of revelation.

## 55. How should the disciples of Jesus live?

As Jesus' disciples we should model ourselves on him, until he is formed in us *(see Ga 4:19)*. As we come ever closer to him, we are made like him. We hope to die and rise with him, until we reign with him in heaven.

## 56. What is the significance of Jesus' temptations?

The temptations in the wilderness show Jesus as the humble Messiah who triumphs over Satan by his complete faithfulness to God's plan of salvation.

## 57. What is the Kingdom of God?

The Kingdom of God (or Kingdom of Heaven), was brought about on earth by Jesus Christ. It is clearly shown to us in the words, work and person of Jesus. The Church is the seed and the beginning of this Kingdom. The keys of the Kingdom are entrusted to Peter and to his successors.

**58. What was the purpose of the Transfiguration?**
The Transfiguration was to strengthen the faith of the apostles prior to the Passion. The ascent of Mount Tabor prepares for the ascent of Calvary. The Transfiguration is a sign of the glory that would follow the Cross, and is a foretaste of the sacraments that are for us the hope of glory.

**59. Did Jesus undergo the Passion freely?**
Jesus went up to Jerusalem freely, knowing that he would die at the hands of sinners.

"JESUS CHRIST SUFFERED UNDER PONTIUS PILATE,
HE WAS CRUCIFIED, DIED AND WAS BURIED"

**60. Why did Jesus encounter opposition from some of the Jews?**
Some of the things Jesus did - such as forgiving sins, expelling demons, healing on the Sabbath day, showing friendship to public sinners - were signs of contradiction. Though these actions showed him to be Saviour, there were those who interpreted what he said and did as blasphemy, because, they said, he made himself out to be God *(cf. Jn 10:33)*.

**61. What is the meaning of the Last Supper?**
Jesus freely gave himself for our salvation on the altar of the Cross. At the Last Supper, he both symbolised

this offering and made it really present: "This is my body, given for you" *(Lk 22:19)*.

## 62. What does it mean to say that Jesus died for our sins?

When we say that Jesus died for our sins, we mean that "in Christ, God was reconciling the world to himself" *(2 Co 5:19)*. God "loved us and sent his Son to be the expiation for our sins" *(1 Jn 4:10)*. Thus our salvation comes from God's love for us.

## 63. What is Christ's Redemption?

Christ's redemptive act was "to give his life as a ransom for many" *(Mt 20:28)*. "He loved his own who were in the world, he loved them to the end" *(Jn 13:1)*, so that they might be "ransomed from the futile ways inherited from their fathers" *(1 P 1:18)*.

## 64. Has Jesus taken away our sins?

Through his loving obedience to the Father, "even to death on the cross" *(Ph 2:8)*, Jesus fulfilled the saving mission of the Suffering Servant which justifies many, by taking their sins upon himself *(cf. Is 53:11)*. In his human nature Jesus is the head of all humankind, and is therefore able to offer his redemptive sacrifice for all.

**65. When Jesus' soul and body were separated by death, were they still united with his divinity?**

Whilst Jesus remained in the tomb, his soul and his body remained united to his divine Person, even though separated by his death.

"JESUS CHRIST DESCENDED INTO HELL,
ON THE THIRD DAY HE ROSE AGAIN FROM THE DEAD"

**66. What does the descent into hell mean?**

By the expression "Jesus descended into hell", the Creed professes that Jesus was truly dead, and that, by dying for us, he had conquered death and the devil who is the one "who has the power of death" *(Heb 2:14)*.

**67. Is the "descent into hell" only a metaphor?**

The descent into hell means that, in his human soul united to his divine Person, the dead Christ truly descended into the realm of the dead, and opened the gate of heaven to the just who had gone before him.

**68. What happened after Jesus died?**

After three days the Lord Jesus rose from the dead. This is called the Resurrection.

**69. Is the Resurrection an historical event?**

The Resurrection of Christ is a real event. The writers of the New Testament bear witness to the historical circumstances of Christ's resurrection. The disciples met

the Lord after he had risen and also witnessed the empty
tomb. However, until he had revealed himself to them
they did not recognise him *(cf. Lk 24:13-35, Jn 20:11-
18)*. The essence of the Resurrection, the passover of
Jesus to another life, transcends and surpasses history
and lies at the heart of the mystery of faith.

**70. What does the empty tomb mean?**
The empty tomb is the first visible indication of the
Resurrection. Along with the cloths thrown on the
ground, it pointed to the fact that the Body of Christ
had, by God's power, escaped from the bonds of
death and corruption. This prepared the disciples for
their meeting with the risen Lord.

**71. Was the resurrection of Christ a return to
earthly life?**
The Resurrection was not the return of Christ to earthly
life. In his risen body, he passed from death to a new
life beyond time and space. His body, though real and
authentic, is now a glorified body.

**72. Is Jesus' resurrection of continued importance
for us?**
Jesus' resurrection is significant for our own salvation.
Christ, "the first-born of those risen from the dead" *(Col
1:18)*, is the guarantee of our own resurrection. Here
and now it is a sign of our justification, and enables us

to rise from sin. It is also the promise that, at the end of time, we will be given new bodily life *(see n. 121)*.

## "HE ASCENDED INTO HEAVEN AND IS SEATED AT THE RIGHT HAND OF GOD THE FATHER ALMIGHTY"

### 73. What did Jesus do after he had risen from the dead?

After he had risen from the dead, the Lord appeared to his disciples until the time came for him to ascend to heaven.

### 74. What does the Ascension mean?

The Ascension marks the definitive entrance of the humanity of Jesus into the heavenly kingdom of God, from where he will return.

### 75. Is Jesus' ascension into heaven important for us?

Jesus Christ, the Head of the Church, has gone before us to the glorious kingdom of the Father so that we, the members of his Body, may hope one day to be united eternally with him.

### 76. Does Jesus Christ, now living in heaven, concern himself with us?

Jesus Christ, having gone once and for all into the sanctuary of heaven, intercedes for us unceasingly, and so assures us of the continual outpouring of the Holy Spirit.

## "FROM WHENCE HE WILL COME TO JUDGE THE LIVING AND THE DEAD"

### 77. Has the reign of Christ already begun?

Christ the Lord reigns already through the Church, though not everything in this world is yet subjected to him. Indeed, the triumph of Christ's kingdom will not come about without one final assault by the powers of evil *(see n. 443)*.

### 78. How long will the struggle between good and evil last?

At the end of the world, on the Day of Judgement, Christ will come in glory to complete the final triumph of good over evil, which, like the wheat and the darnel of the parable *(Mt 13:24-30)*, will grow together during the course of history.

### 79. What will happen on the Day of Judgement?

Christ in glory, coming at the end of time to judge the living and the dead, will reveal the secrets of the heart and will give to everyone according to their works, and according to how they have welcomed or refused God's grace and love *(see n. 133)*.

## THE HOLY SPIRIT

"I BELIEVE IN THE HOLY SPIRIT"

### 80. Who is the Holy Spirit?

The Holy Spirit is the third Person of the Blessed Trinity, the one whom the Father has sent into our hearts, the Spirit of his Son. He is truly God, the Lord and Giver of Life. He proceeds from the Father and the Son; with the Father and the Son he is worshipped and glorified.

### 81. What was the role of the Holy Spirit in the Incarnation of the Son?

In the fullness of time, the Holy Spirit brought to fulfilment in Mary all the preparations made for the coming of Christ among the people of Israel. Through the work of the Holy Spirit in her, the Father gave to the world the Emmanuel, "God with us" *(Mt 1:23)*. The Son of God is consecrated as the Christ, the Messiah, by the anointing of the Holy Spirit at his baptism in the Jordan by John *(cf. Mk 1:10, Ac 10:37-38) (see n. 40)*.

### 82. How was the Holy Spirit first given to the Church?

The Holy Spirit was first given to the Church at Pentecost, when the apostles "were all filled with the Holy Spirit" *(Ac 2:4)*. Since that time, from his place of glory with the Father, Christ continues to pour out the gift of the Holy Spirit on the faithful in a variety of ways. This gift builds, animates and sanctifies the whole Church *(see nn. 409, 413)*.

## 83. In what particular ways is the Holy Spirit given to us?

The Holy Spirit is given to us especially through the sacraments and in particular through Baptism and Confirmation. There are also special marks of the presence of the Holy Spirit in our lives through what are called charisms. These are gifts of office and state of life, for example, teaching, prophesying, caring for those in need, living as a religious, bringing up children. "Our gifts differ according to the grace given us" *(Rm 12:6)*.

"I BELIEVE IN THE HOLY CATHOLIC CHURCH"

## 84. What is the Church?

The word "Church" means "assembly". It describes the liturgical assembly of those whom the Word of God gathers together to form the People of God. It also refers to both the local community and to the universal community of believers. The Church is thus the People that God gathers in the whole world. This People, nourished by the Word, and by the Body of Christ in the sacrament of the Eucharist, themselves become the Body of Christ.

## 85. When did the Church begin and how long will it continue?

The Church is both the means and the end of God's plan. The Church was at the heart of God's creative purposes from the beginning. She was prepared for in the Old Covenant, founded by the words and actions of Jesus Christ, established by his saving cross and his resurrection, and revealed as the mystery of salvation by the outpouring of the Holy Spirit at Pentecost. She will come to completion in the glory of heaven as the assembly of all the redeemed.

## 86. Is the Church visible?

The Church is both visible and spiritual. She is a hierarchical society and the Mystical Body of Christ. She is "one", made of a human and of a divine element. This is her mystery, which only faith can grasp.

## 87. Why is the Church important?

The Church in this world is the sacrament of salvation. She is the sign and instrument of the communion of God with all his people.

## 88. How does one become a member of the Church?

One comes into the Church through faith and Baptism (see n. 147 ff.).

**89. What are the principal names given to the Church?**

The principal names of the Church are: the People of God, the Body and Bride of Christ, the Temple of the Holy Spirit. The Universal Church shows herself as a People gathered together in the unity of Father, Son and Holy Spirit.

**90. Why is the Church called the "People of God"?**

The members of the Church are called the People of God because God has chosen them in a special way: "You are a chosen race, a royal priesthood, a holy nation, God's own people" *(1 P 2:9)*.

**91. Why is the Church called the "Body of Christ"?**

The Church is called the Body of Christ to indicate the intimate relationship between Christ and the Church. Through the Holy Spirit and his actions in the sacraments, above all in the Eucharist, the risen Christ establishes the community of the faithful as his Body, with him as the Head. All the members, different among themselves and with different functions, are bound one to the other, particularly to those who are suffering, poor and persecuted.

**92. Why is the Church called the "Bride of Christ"?**
The Church is the Bride of Christ because he loved her and gave himself for her. He purified her in his blood. He made her Mother of all the children of God.

**93. Why is the Church called the "Temple of the Holy Spirit"?**
The Church is called the Temple of the Holy Spirit because the Holy Spirit is, as it were, the soul of the Mystical Body. The Holy Spirit is the source of its life, of its unity in diversity, and of the richness of its gifts and charisms *(see nn. 409, 413)*.

**94. What are the basic characteristics of the Church?**
The fundamental characteristics of the Church are its four marks, inextricably linked to each other: the Church is One, Holy, Catholic and Apostolic.

**95. How is the Church one?**
The Church is one because she has only one Lord, professes one faith, gives birth through one baptism, is one Body, is made alive by one and the same Spirit, and holds to the one hope in God. The Church believes that, when all is fulfilled, everything will be made one in Christ and divisions will be ended.

## 96. Is the Church completely one?

In the one and only Church of God, from the very beginning there were certain divisions. These divisions wound the visible unity of Christ's Body. The ecumenical movement encourages the healing of the wounds of disunity.

## 97. What of those who follow Christ but do not belong to the Catholic Church?

"All who have been justified by faith in baptism are incorporated into Christ; they therefore have a right to be called Christians, and with good reason are accepted as brothers and sisters in the Lord by the children of the Catholic Church" *(Vat. II: UR 3 § 1)*.

## 98. How is the Church holy?

The Church is holy because she is created by the most holy God. Christ, her Bridegroom, gave himself up for her to make her holy. The Spirit of holiness gives her life. Even though she contains sinful people, the Church is without spot or stain. Her glory shines forth in all the saints and especially in Mary in whom is found all holiness.

## 99. How is the Church catholic?

The Church is catholic because she proclaims the whole faith. She has within herself and administers the fullness of the means of salvation. By her very nature

she is missionary, and is sent to all people. She speaks
to people of every race and nation, in every age.

## 100. How is the Church apostolic?

The Church is apostolic because she is built on firm
foundations, the twelve Apostles of the Lamb *(Rv
21:14)*. Christ himself governs the Church through
Peter and the other Apostles who are present in their
successors, the Pope and the bishops. Hence the
Church is indestructibly and infallibly preserved in
the truth *(see n. 205)*.

## 101. Why is the Church called the "ark of salvation"?

All salvation comes from Christ the Head, through his
Body, the Church. Hence the Church is destined as
the home for all the saved. However, those who,
through no fault of their own, do not know the Gospel
of Christ and his Church, but who sincerely search for
God and try to do his will, may indeed achieve eternal
salvation. In their journey towards salvation they act
under the influence of God's grace *(see n. 152)*.

## 102. What of those who belong to other faiths?

Foremost among these are the Jews - the Law, the
prophets, and the Old Covenant belong to them; Jesus
was himself born into a Jewish family. Muslims
acknowledge the Creator, hold to the faith of Abraham,

and adore the one, merciful God. In many other
religions there are those who search for the God who is
both unknown yet near, since he gives life and breath to
all. God wants all people to be saved.

### 103. How is the Church structured?

Jesus says, "I am the vine, you are the branches" *(Jn
15:5)*. The Church is the vine, and its members are the
branches. The members consist of laity, clergy and
religious. The lay faithful *(laity)* are those who have
become members of the Church through Baptism. From
among these, by divine institution, men are chosen to
serve as bishops, priests, and deacons *(clergy)*. There
are also those who profess the evangelical counsels,
and are consecrated to God in a special way *(religious)*.

### 104. Has the Church a visible foundation?

The Lord made Peter the visible foundation of his
Church, and he gave him "the power of the keys". The
successor of Peter in his mission is the Pope, the bishop
of Rome, who is the head of the College of Bishops.

### 105. What is the power of the keys given to Peter and his successors?

By divine institution, the Pope is vested with supreme,
full, immediate and universal power for the good of
souls. He enjoys the prerogative of infallibility when

he proclaims by a definitive act a doctrine concerning faith or morals.

### 106. Who are the bishops?

The bishops, through the power of the Holy Spirit, are the successors of the apostles. On their own, they are the visible sign and source of unity in their dioceses, or local churches *(see n. 205)*.

### 107. What is the work of a bishop?

Bishops, helped by priests and deacons, have as their principal tasks: to teach the faith authentically; to celebrate the liturgy, and above all the Eucharist; and to guide the Church as true pastors. An integral part of their office is care of all the churches, with and under the Pope.

### 108. Who are the lay faithful (the laity)?

"The laity are the community of the faithful on earth under the leadership of the Pope and of the bishops in communion with him. They are the Church" *(CL 9)*.

### 109. What is the calling of the laity?

The laity are called to live in the world and, through their daily work, to exercise their apostolate like leaven, thus responding to the call to holiness of all the baptised. By virtue of their baptism and confirmation they share in Christ's royal, prophetic and priestly work.

## 110. Who are the religious?

Religious are those who have made a public profession of the evangelical counsels of poverty, chastity and obedience, in a stable form of life, recognised by the Church.

## 111. What are the qualities of a religious?

All the baptised are already bound to God by love. As religious are consecrated to God by public vows, they are thereby intimately consecrated to divine service and dedicated to the good of all the Church.

## 112 .What is the communion of saints?

The communion of saints is the Church. The phrase has two closely linked meanings. It refers to a communion in "holy things", and in particular to the Eucharist, the sign and source of the unity of all the faithful. It also refers to a communion among "holy people", so that what each does for Christ bears fruit for all.

## 113. Does the name "communion of saints" refer only to those here on earth?

We believe in the communion of all the faithful in Christ: those who are pilgrims here on earth, the dead who are still undergoing a purification, and the blessed in heaven. All of these form one Church. We believe that, in this communion, the merciful love of God and the saints is for ever listening to our prayers *(see nn. 416, 439)*.

## 114. What is the role of Mary in the work of our redemption?

In pronouncing her *fiat* at the Annunciation, and in giving her consent to the mystery of the Incarnation, Mary was already collaborating in her Son's work. Jesus is Saviour and Head of his Mystical Body; on the cross he gave Mary to us as our Mother *(see nn. 53, 414)*.

## 115. How did Mary's life on earth end?

When her life on earth was completed, Mary was raised in body and soul to heaven, where she shares in the glory of her Son's resurrection, anticipating in herself the resurrection of all the members of his Body. This is known as the Assumption of Our Lady into heaven.

## 116. Is Our Lady concerned about us now?

The Blessed Mother of God, the new Eve, Mother of the Church, continues her maternal role in heaven in relation to all the members of Christ's Body, the Church.

"I BELIEVE IN THE FORGIVENESS OF SIN"

## 117. Why does the Creed speak of the remission of sins at this stage?

The Creed connects the forgiveness of sin to the profession of faith in the Holy Spirit. The risen Christ gave the power to forgive sins to the apostles when he gave them the Holy Spirit.

THE PROFESSION OF CHRISTIAN FAITH 41

## 118. How are our sins forgiven?

Our sins are forgiven initially and principally through Baptism. This unites us to the risen Christ, and gives us the Holy Spirit.

## 119. Apart from Baptism, are there other ways in which our sins are forgiven?

True sorrow for sin brings forgiveness. In accordance with Christ's will, the Church has the power to forgive those sins committed after Baptism. This power is exercised by bishops and priests, through the sacraments of Penance and the Anointing of the Sick *(see nn. 179 ff.)*. The Eucharist is also a means of forgiveness *(see n. 187)*.

### "I BELIEVE IN THE RESURRECTION OF THE BODY"

## 120. Does the Church value the whole of creation?

The Church gives great value to the whole of creation. We believe in God, the creator of all things; we believe in the Word made Flesh given for the redemption of all flesh; we believe in the resurrection of the body; and we believe in the fulfilment of all creation at the end of time.

## 121. What will happen to our mortal bodies?

At death the soul is separated from the body, but on the Last Day at the resurrection, body and soul will be reunited, and God will give an incorruptible life to our transformed bodies. As Christ is risen and lives for ever, so we too will all rise on the last day *(see n. 72)*.

**122. Will our risen bodies be the same as the bodies we now have?**
We believe in the resurrection of the body that we now have. However, whilst our natural body is corruptible, our risen bodies will be incorruptible *(1 Co 15:44)*.

**123. Why do we have to die?**
All humanity is subject to bodily death because of original sin. If it were not for original sin we would not have to die *(see n. 37)*.

**124. What does death mean to a Christian?**
For the Christian, death has a positive meaning. The obedience of Jesus has transformed the curse of death into a blessing. "For to me to live is Christ, and to die is gain" *(Ph 1:21)*, says St Paul. "I shall not die, but enter into life", says St Thérèse of Lisieux.

**125 How should we prepare for death?**
The Church encourages us to prepare ourselves for the hour of our death ("From an unprovided death, deliver us, O Lord", *The Litany of the Saints*). We should ask the Mother of God to intercede for us "at the hour of our death" *(Hail Mary)*, and entrust ourselves to St Joseph, patron of a good death.

"I BELIEVE IN ETERNAL LIFE"

## 126. What happens immediately after death?

Immediately after death, each person is judged by Christ. The immortal soul receives a just reward according to how that person has lived, and enters heaven, purgatory or hell. This particular judgement is the work of Christ, judge of the living and of the dead.

## 127. What is heaven?

Heaven is the state in which we see God face to face, are made like him in glory, and enjoy eternal happiness. It is the communion of life and love with the Blessed Trinity, with Mary, the angels and all the saints. It is the fulfilment of all our longings. "Things that no eye has seen and no ear has heard, things beyond the mind of man, all that God has prepared for those who love him" *(1 Co 2:9)*.

## 128. What do those who are now in Paradise do?

We believe that the souls that are reunited with Jesus and Mary in Paradise form the Church of heaven. They are eternally blessed and see God as he is. They are also associated with the holy angels, interceding for us and helping our weakness with their loving care.

**129. What is purgatory?**

Purgatory is the state of those who die in the grace and friendship of God, but who are not yet fully purified. Although these souls are certain of eternal salvation, they undergo a period of purification so that they may attain the holiness necessary to enter into the glory of God.

**130. What does the Church do for these souls?**

Through the communion of saints, the Church commends the souls in purgatory to the mercy of God, and offers prayers, especially the eucharistic sacrifice, for them *(see n. 193)*.

**131. What is hell?**

Hell is the state of eternal punishment for those who have died in mortal sin without repenting and accepting God's merciful love. Following the example of Christ, who speaks of "eternal fire", the Church warns the faithful of the awful and painful reality of hell *(see n. 272)*.

**132. What is the principal pain of hell?**

The principal pain of hell is eternal separation from God. Only in God can we find the life and happiness for which we are created and to which we aspire.

**133. At the end of time, after the final resurrection, will everyone appear before Christ the judge?**

The Church firmly believes and teaches that on the Day of Judgement everyone will appear with their own bodies before the tribunal of Christ, to give an account of their lives. This is the Last (or General) Judgement *(see n. 79)*.

**134. How does the General Judgement differ from the Particular Judgement?**

The Particular Judgement concerns the individual human soul, whereas the General Judgement concerns the whole human race. On the Last Day, God, through his Son Jesus Christ, will pronounce the final word on all history. We shall know the ultimate meaning of God's works of creation and salvation, and understand the marvellous way in which Providence has brought everything to its final end.

**135. What will be the end of everything?**

At the end of time, the Kingdom of God will come to its completion. Then the just will reign with Christ for ever, glorified in body and soul, and the material universe will itself be transformed. There will be a new heaven and a new earth, and God will be "all in all" *(1 Co 15:28)* in eternal life *(see n. 443)*.

The Good Shepherd, lunette from above the entrance, mid 5th century (mosaic). Mausoleo di Galla Placidia, Ravenna, Italy.

# PART TWO

## ❧ THE CELEBRATION OF THE ❧ CHRISTIAN MYSTERY

### THE CELEBRATION OF THE CHRISTIAN MYSTERY: PART 2, §§ 1066-1690

**Sacraments and the Liturgy:**
**Section 1, §§ 1066-1209**

**The Seven Sacraments of the Church:**
**Section 2, §§ 1210-1690**

• The Sacraments of Christian initiation: Chapter 1, §§ 1212-1419.

• The Sacraments of healing: Chapter 2, §§ 1420-1532.

• Sacraments at the service of communion: Chapter 3, §§ 1533-1666.

• Other Liturgical celebrations: Chapter 4, §§ 1667-1690.

# – ❧ SACRAMENTS AND LITURGY ❧ –

## 136. What are the sacraments?

The sacraments are efficacious signs of grace, instituted by Christ and entrusted to the Church, through which God lavishes upon us a share in his divine life. The visible rites by which the sacraments are celebrated signify and make present the graces proper to each sacrament. They bear fruit in those who are properly disposed to receive them *(see nn. 306, 308, 310).*

## 137. Why are the sacraments called sacraments of faith?

They are called sacraments of faith because they pre-suppose faith, nourish it, strengthen it and express it, through the words and actions of the rites.

## 138. Are the sacraments necessary for salvation?

The Church affirms that, for believers, the sacraments of the New Covenant are necessary for salvation.

## 139 What is sacramental grace?

Sacramental grace is the grace of the Holy Spirit given by Christ which is proper to each sacrament.

## 140. How are the sacraments administered?

The sacraments are administered through the Church's public worship, called the liturgy. The liturgy is the work of the whole Christ, Head and members.

**141. Who is the first celebrant of the liturgy?**

The first celebrant of the liturgy is Christ himself. As High Priest he celebrates the heavenly liturgy ceaselessly in the presence of the holy Mother of God, the apostles, the saints and all those who are already in the Kingdom.

**142. Who among us celebrates the liturgy?**

All those present at a liturgical celebration take part in the liturgy. Every member of the Body of Christ shares in the priesthood of the baptised, but some of the faithful are ordained through the sacrament of Orders to represent Christ as Head of the Body *(see n. 201)*.

**143. What is the Lord's Day?**

The Lord's Day is Sunday, the day on which Jesus rose from the dead. It is the most appropriate day for the liturgical assembly and the Eucharist. It is the day for the Christian family. It is a day of joy, of rest from work and of recreation. It is the foundation and basis of the whole liturgical year. It is a weekly celebration of Christ's resurrection *(see nn. 339-341)*.

**144. What is the Liturgical Year?**

The Liturgical Year is the annual cycle in which the Church unfolds the whole mystery of Christ, from his Incarnation and Birth, through his Passion, Death, Resurrection and Ascension, to the day of Pentecost, waiting "in joyful hope for the coming of our Saviour, Jesus Christ" *(from the Communion Rite at Mass) (see n. 420)*.

# THE SEVEN SACRAMENTS
## ❧ OF THE CHURCH ❧

**145. How many sacraments are there and what are they called?**

The sacraments of the Church, instituted by Jesus Christ, number seven. They are: *Baptism*, *Confirmation*, the *Eucharist*, *Penance*, the *Anointing of the Sick*, *Holy Orders* and *Marriage*.

**146. How are the seven sacraments grouped?**

The sacraments are grouped into the sacraments of Christian initiation (Baptism, Confirmation, the Eucharist), the sacraments of healing (Penance and the Anointing of the Sick), and those which are at the service of communion and the mission of the faithful (Holy Orders and Marriage). However, the Eucharist occupies a unique place in the sacramental system as the 'Sacrament of sacraments' since it contains the whole spiritual good of the Church, namely Christ himself. For this reason all other sacraments are related to it as to their centre.

### THE SACRAMENTS OF CHRISTIAN INITIATION

#### BAPTISM

**147. How is Christian initiation brought about?**

An individual is initiated as a Christian through three sacraments: Baptism, which is the beginning of new life; Confirmation, which is its strengthening; and the Eucharist, which nourishes with the Body and Blood of Christ so as to make the Christian disciple more like Christ.

## 148. Why is Baptism important?

Baptism is important because it brings the individual to a new life in Christ and to membership of the Church. According to the will of the Lord it is necessary for salvation, as is belonging to the Church.

## 149. What is the essential feature of the baptismal rite?

The essential feature of the baptismal rite is immersing the candidate three times in water, or pouring water three times over the person's head, while saying: "[N], I baptise you in the name of the Father and of the Son and of the Holy Spirit".

## 150. What is the fruit of Baptism?

Baptismal grace, the first fruit of this sacrament, is a rich reality which carries with it a number of distinct effects. Among these is the remission of original sin and of all personal sins. Moreover, the individual is born to new life, and so becomes an adopted child of the Father, a member of Christ, and a temple of the Holy Spirit. In addition, the newly baptised becomes a member of the Church, and shares in the priesthood of Christ *(see nn. 38, 88)*.

## 151. Can Baptism be repeated?

Baptism imprints on the soul an indelible mark, or character, which consecrates the baptised for Christian worship. Because of this character, Baptism cannot be repeated.

## 152. Is it possible to be saved without Baptism?

Those who are martyred because of their faith, catechumens, and all those who, moved by grace, sincerely search for God and try to do his will, may also be saved, even though they are not baptised *(see n. 101)*.

## 153. Can Baptism be administered to children?

From the earliest times, Baptism has been administered to children, as a grace and gift of God which does not depend on human merit. The children are baptised in the faith of the Church. Entry into Christian life leads to true freedom.

## 154. What of children who die without Baptism?

With respect to children who die without Baptism, the Church's liturgy invites us to have faith in God's mercy and to pray for their salvation.

## 155. Who can baptise?

In case of necessity, anyone may baptise who intends to do what the Church does.

CONFIRMATION

## 156. What is Confirmation?

Confirmation is the sacrament that perfects the grace of Baptism. It gives the Holy Spirit so as to root us more deeply in our relationship with God as his sons and daughters, to incorporate us more solidly in Christ, to strengthen our link with the Church by associating us more closely in her mission, and to help us witness to the Christian faith in word and deed.

## 157. Can Confirmation be repeated?

Like Baptism, Confirmation imprints on the Christian's soul an indelible spiritual mark or character. It can thus be received only once.

## 158. When is Confirmation conferred?

In the Latin Church, Confirmation is normally conferred on those who have attained the age of reason.

## 159. Who can administer Confirmation?

Confirmation is normally administered by the bishop, showing clearly that its effect is to unite those who receive it more closely with the Church.

## 160. What is required of those being confirmed?

Candidates for Confirmation who have attained the age of reason must profess the faith, be in a state of grace, intend to receive the sacrament, and be prepared to take on the responsibilities of being both disciples and witnesses to Christ, both in the Church and in their daily lives.

### 161. What is the essential rite of the sacrament?

The essential rite of Confirmation is the anointing with chrism on the forehead of the baptised, accompanied by the imposition of hands by the minister, who says: "Be sealed with the gift of the Holy Spirit".

### 162. How is the link between Baptism and Confirmation expressed?

When Confirmation is celebrated separately from Baptism, its link with it is expressed by the renewal of the baptismal promises. Above all, the celebration of Confirmation during Mass serves to underline the unity of the sacraments of Christian initiation *(see n. 147)*.

THE EUCHARIST

### 163. What is the Eucharist?

The Eucharist is the sacrament of Christ's Body and Blood instituted at the Last Supper. It perpetuates the sacrifice of the cross for all time. It completes the process of Christian initiation begun by Baptism and developed by Confirmation by enabling the Christian to share in Christ's own sacrifice and life. It is the life-giving food for the Christian's journey *(see Jn 6)*.

**164. Is the Eucharist called by any other names?**
The unfathomable richness of this sacrament is
indicated by the variety of names given to it, among
which are: the Eucharist, the Lord's Supper, the
Breaking of Bread, the Eucharistic Assembly, the
Holy Sacrifice, the Holy and Divine Liturgy, Holy
Communion, Holy Mass.

**165. How is the Eucharist celebrated?**
The celebration of the Eucharist always includes the
following: the proclamation of the Word of God;
thanksgiving to God the Father for his blessings and
above all for the gift of his Son; the consecration of the
bread and wine; and the sharing in the liturgical banquet
through receiving the Body and Blood of the Lord.
These elements constitute one single act of worship.

**166. What is the place of the Eucharist in the life of
the Church?**
The Eucharist is the source and summit of the life of
the Church, because in it Christ associates his Church
and all her members with his own sacrifice of praise
and thanksgiving offered to the Father once and for all
on the cross. The grace of salvation is poured out on
the Church, Christ's Body, through this sacrifice.

**167. What is the link between the Eucharist and
Christ's Passover?**
The Eucharist is the memorial of Christ's Passover,
that is, of the work of salvation accomplished through

the life, death and resurrection of Christ, a work made present by the liturgical celebration.

## 168. Who offers the eucharistic sacrifice?

It is Christ, the eternal priest of the New Covenant, acting through the ministry of priests, who offers the eucharistic sacrifice. It is the same Christ, really present under the forms of bread and wine, who offers himself in this sacrifice.

## 169. Who can consecrate the Eucharist?

Only validly ordained priests can preside at the Eucharistic Celebration and consecrate the bread and wine so that they become the Body and Blood of the Lord.

## 170. What are the essential signs of the Eucharist?

The essential signs of the Eucharist are wheat bread and grape wine, on which the blessing of the Holy Spirit is invoked and the priest utters the words of consecration said by Jesus during the Last Supper: "This is my body. This is the cup of my blood".

## 171. What happens at the consecration?

At the consecration the bread and wine are changed into the Body and Blood of Christ. Under the form of the consecrated bread and wine, Christ himself, living and glorified, is present truly, really and substantially with his body, blood, soul and divinity. This change is aptly called transubstantiation.

## 172. Is the eucharistic sacrifice solely an act of praise and thanksgiving?

The eucharistic sacrifice is not only an act of praise and thanksgiving, but is offered also in reparation for the sins of the living and the dead, so as to obtain spiritual and temporal blessings from God.

## 173. What are the conditions for receiving Communion worthily?

Those who wish to receive Christ in Holy Communion worthily should be in a state of grace. Someone who is conscious of having sinned mortally should not receive the Eucharist without first having received absolution in the sacrament of Penance, or, if this is not possible and there is a serious need to receive Holy Communion, having made an act of perfect contrition *(see nn. 271, 187)*.

## 174. What are the fruits of worthy reception of the Eucharist?

Worthy reception of Holy Communion leads the recipient to closer union with the Lord, remits venial sin and preserves from grave or mortal sin. Moreover it strengthens the bonds of charity between the recipient and Christ. The Eucharist strengthens the unity of the Church.

## 175. When may Holy Communion be received?

The Church strongly recommends that the faithful who are rightly disposed should receive Holy Communion whenever they attend Holy Mass. They are obliged to receive at least once a year *(see nn. 173, 318)*.

## 176. May Christians who are not Catholics ever receive Holy Communion?

The Catholic Church sees a profound connection between the Eucharist and the Church, and regards the first reception of this sacrament as the climax of entry into the Church. For this reason Catholic discipline normally reserves the Eucharist (and the sacraments of Penance and Anointing of the Sick) to Catholics. However, it is 'a source of joy' that, in special circumstances, and under certain specified conditions, other Christians may be invited to these sacraments. Like all who receive this sacrament, they should be properly disposed *(see Ut Unum Sint, n. 46)*.

## 177. May one adore the Eucharist?

Since Christ himself is really present in the Eucharist, it is necessary to honour him in it with the worship of adoration. The Eucharist is reserved in churches to encourage worship. The reserved sacrament is known as the Blessed Sacrament. To visit the Blessed Sacrament is a mark of recognition of Christ the Lord, a sign of love, and an indication of gratitude.

## 178. What is the connection between the Eucharist and eternal life?

Since Christ has passed from this world to the Father, the Eucharist is a pledge for us of future glory with him. Sharing in this Holy Sacrifice makes us one with Christ, sustains our strength during life's pilgrimage, makes us yearn for eternal life, and unites us to the Church in heaven, with our Lady and all the saints.

### THE SACRAMENTS OF HEALING

#### THE SACRAMENT OF PENANCE OR OF RECONCILIATION

## 179. How can we obtain forgiveness for those sins committed after Baptism?

The forgiveness of sins committed after Baptism is obtained through the sacrament of Penance. This sacrament is also called the sacrament of Conversion, of Confession, and of Reconciliation.

## 180. When did Jesus speak of this sacrament?

After his resurrection, the Lord Jesus showed himself to his apostles and said to them: "Receive the Holy Spirit. If you forgive the sins of any, they are forgiven them; if you retain the sins of any, they are retained" *(Jn 20:22-23)*.

### 181. Why is sin such a great evil?

Sin wounds God's honour and his love. It is against the true dignity of those called to be children of God. It spoils the spiritual health of the Church, within which every Christian ought to become an active member *(see nn. 271, 272)*.

### 182. Is there an evil greater than sin itself?

To a person of faith there is no evil greater than sin. Nothing has worse consequences for the sinner, and for the Church, and indeed for the whole world *(see nn. 271, 272)*.

### 183. What must one do to return to God?

The way back to God, called conversion or repentance, requires sorrow, detestation for the sin committed, and a firm purpose of amendment. Conversion looks both to the future and the past; it is nourished by hope in divine mercy *(see n. 312)*.

### 184. Does repentance depend solely on the individual?

Having fallen into sin, returning to communion with God is a movement born of God's grace. God is full of mercy and care for the salvation of everyone. We must ask for the precious gift of conversion for ourselves and for others *(see n. 304)*.

**185. What are the basic elements of the sacrament of Penance?**

The sacrament of Penance consists of three acts performed by the penitent, together with absolution given by the priest. The penitential acts are: repentance (sorrow for our sins), confession to the priest (admission of our sins), and the intention to complete whatever is required by way of satisfaction (making amends for our sins).

**186. What should the motives for contrition be?**

Contrition (also called repentance) ought to be inspired by motives arising out of faith. All contrition is a gift of God, prompted by the Holy Spirit. If contrition is born solely out of love for God's goodness it is called "perfect".

**187. Is it possible to obtain forgiveness for grave sin through anything other than this sacrament?**

Individual and complete confession of all grave sin, followed by absolution from a priest, are the ordinary means for reconciliation with God and with the Church. Nonetheless, someone who has committed a grave sin can obtain forgiveness by making an act of perfect contrition, coupled with a firm resolution to have recourse as soon as possible to sacramental confession *(see n. 173)*.

**188. What sins ought to be confessed?**

One who wishes to be reconciled to God and to the Church should make a careful examination of conscience and then confess to a priest all the grave sins thus recalled that have not previously been confessed. It is helpful (though not necessary) if venial sins are also confessed *(see nn. 270-273)*.

**189. Why is it necessary to make satisfaction?**

The acts of satisfaction (the penance) which the priest suggests to the penitent are to repair the damage caused by the sin, and to restore and strengthen those habits (called virtues) proper to one of Christ's disciples.

**190. Can any priest give absolution?**

Only a priest who has received faculties from the Church (that is, who has jurisdiction) can normally give absolution.

**191. What are the spiritual effects of the sacrament of Penance?**

There are many spiritual effects of the sacrament of Penance. *(a)* Reconciliation with God through which the penitent recovers grace. *(b)* Reconciliation with the Church. *(c)* Remission of the eternal penalties deserved by mortal sin. *(d)* The remission, at least in part, of the temporal penalty incurred by sin. *(e)* The peace and serenity of a good conscience and spiritual consolation. *(f)* Growth in spiritual strength gained through the Christian struggle.

## 192. Are there different ways in which the sacrament of Penance may be celebrated?

The Church proposes three ways in which the sacrament of Penance may be celebrated. The most common form is individual confession to a priest followed by absolution. A second form is the celebration of a service of Penance at which individual confession and absolution are a part. A third form allows, in certain rare circumstances, general confession and absolution.

## 193. What is an indulgence?

An indulgence is a remission in God's sight of the temporal punishment due to sins whose guilt has already been forgiven. Every indulgence is derived from the treasury of merits of Christ and the saints. Someone who is well disposed and who fulfils the conditions laid down, may gain an indulgence through the authority of the Church. Indulgences may be partial or plenary. They may also be applied for the benefit of those who have died.

THE ANOINTING OF THE SICK

## 194. What does Scripture say about the Anointing of the Sick?

The apostle James says: "If one of you is ill, he should send for the elders of the church, and they must anoint him with oil in the name of the Lord and pray over him. The prayer of faith will save the sick man and the Lord will raise him up again; and if he has committed any sins, he will be forgiven" *(Jm 5:14-15)*.

## 195. What is the effect of this sacrament?

The sacrament of the Anointing of the Sick has the power to confer a special grace on the Christian who is experiencing the hardships that belong to serious sickness or old age.

## 196. What is the special grace of this sacrament?

The special graces of the sacrament of the sick are: *(a)* the union of the sick person with the Passion of Christ, for the benefit of that person, and for the good of the whole Church; *(b)* the granting of comfort, peace and courage to enable the person to endure the sufferings of sickness or old age; *(c)* the forgiveness of sin (if the sick person has not been able to receive the sacrament of Penance); *(d)* the recovery of health, if this will assist the person's salvation; and *(e)* preparation for the journey to eternal life.

## 197. When should this sacrament be received?

The Anointing of the Sick is for those faithful who begin to find themselves in some danger of death through sickness or old age, and is by no means only for those at the point of death.

## 198. How often may this sacrament be received?

Every time Christians fall gravely sick they may receive this holy anointing, especially when, although they have already been anointed, the sickness grows worse.

## 199. How is the sacrament of the Anointing of the sick administered?

Only priests can confer the sacrament of the Anointing of the Sick. The oil to be used is that blessed by the bishop (at the Chrism Mass during Holy Week) or, if necessary, by the priest himself. The forehead and the hands of the sick person are anointed, accompanied by prayer in which the priest pleads for the special grace of the sacrament.

## 200. What is Viaticum?

Viaticum is the Eucharist given to someone who is about to die; it is so called because it is food for the journey *(via)*. The Eucharist is here the sacrament of passing over from death to life, from this world to the Father. The Church offers the Eucharist as Viaticum at this important moment because it is the seed of eternal life and the power of resurrection. Thus, just as the sacraments of Baptism, Confirmation and the Eucharist form a unity called 'the sacraments of initiation', so it can be said that Penance, the Anointing of the Sick and the Eucharist as Viaticum are, at the end of the Christian's life, 'the sacraments that prepare for our heavenly homeland', or the sacraments that complete the earthly pilgrimage.

## SACRAMENTS AT THE SERVICE OF COMMUNION

### THE SACRAMENT OF ORDERS

### 201. What are the different ways of sharing in the priesthood of Christ?

The whole Church is a priestly people. By virtue of their Baptism, all the faithful share in the priesthood of Christ. Such a sharing is called "the common priesthood of the faithful". On this foundation of service is built a further sharing in Christ's mission, namely the ministry conferred by the sacrament of Orders. By this, someone is given the task of serving the community in the name of and in the person of Christ the Head.

### 202. Why is the ministerial priesthood different from the priesthood of the faithful?

The ministerial priesthood differs essentially from the common priesthood of the faithful because it confers a sacred power for the service of the faithful. Ordained ministers exercise their service through teaching, divine worship and pastoral leadership.

## 203. What are the different degrees in which the ordained ministry is exercised?

Traditionally the ordained ministry is exercised in three degrees: as bishop, priest and deacon.

## 204. Are ordained ministers necessary to the life of the Church?

The ministries conferred by ordination are essential to the proper structure of the Church *(see n. 103)*.

## 205. What is a bishop?

A bishop is one who has received the fullness of the sacrament of Orders, who belongs to the College of Bishops, and who is the visible head of the local Church (the diocese) entrusted to him. As successors of the apostles, bishops have a share in the apostolic duties and mission of the whole Church, under the authority of the Pope, successor of St Peter *(see n. 106)*.

## 206. What are priests?

Priests are those ordained ministers who are called to be the bishops' conscientious fellow-workers. They are united to them in their priestly office, and are dependent on them for the exercise of their pastoral ministry. With their bishop they form the presbyterate, with responsibility for the diocese. Priests are given responsibility by their bishop for a parish community, or for some other special task within the Church.

## 207. What is the particular work of bishops and priests?

Bishops and priests are ordained in particular to proclaim God's word by preaching and teaching, and to celebrate the Eucharist and the other sacraments.

## 208. What are deacons?

Deacons are ministers ordained for the work of service in the Church. While they do not receive the ministerial priesthood, their ordination confers important responsibilities on them for the ministry of the word, for divine worship, for pastoral leadership and for the service of charity. In all this they act under the pastoral authority of their bishop.

## 209. How is the sacrament of Orders conferred?

The sacrament of Orders is conferred by the bishop through the imposition of hands followed by a solemn consecratory prayer that calls on God to grant to the candidate the grace of the Holy Spirit required for his ministry. Ordination gives a sacramental character that cannot be removed.

## 210. Who can be ordained?

The Church confers the sacrament of Orders only on baptised men, whose suitability for the exercise of this ministry has been duly recognised.

## 211. What is the connection between priesthood and celibacy?

In the Latin Church, the sacrament of priestly ordination is normally given only to those who have freely embraced celibacy, and who have made a public sign of their willing acceptance of this state for love of the Kingdom of God and for the service of all.

THE SACRAMENT OF MARRIAGE

## 212. Why is Marriage included among the sacraments?

Christian Marriage is a real and effective sign of the covenant of Christ with the Church. Since it signifies and communicates grace, Marriage between baptised persons is a true sacrament of the New Covenant. "Husbands should love their wives just as Christ loved the Church and sacrificed himself for her" *(Ep 5:25)*.

## 213. Has the marriage covenant its own proper laws?

The marriage covenant, by which a man and a woman form between themselves an intimate communion of

life and of love, is a state founded on and given its
own laws by the Creator. Marriage is for the holiness
of the spouses and for the generation and education of
children. Christ raised Marriage between the baptised
to the dignity of a sacrament *(see nn. 362, 363)*.

## 214. What is the grace of the sacrament of Marriage?

The sacrament of Marriage is a sign of the union
between Christ and the Church. Spouses are given the
grace to love each other with the love by which Christ
has loved the Church. The grace of the sacrament is
intended to perfect the couple's love, to strengthen
their indissoluble union and to sanctify them in their
journey to God *(see nn. 362, 363)*.

## 215. What is the basic element of the sacrament of Marriage?

The indispensable element that makes a marriage is
the consent exchanged between the man and the
woman, that is, their mutual and definitive free self-
giving, in order to live according to a covenant of
faithful and fruitful love *(see nn. 362, 363)*.

## 216. Should the celebration of the sacrament of Marriage be public?

Since Marriage brings the couple into a public position
within the Church, it is appropriate that the celebration

of the sacrament is performed publicly, as part of a liturgical celebration, in the presence of a priest (or of a witness who can represent the Church), of witnesses, and of the body of the faithful.

## 217. What are the essential characteristics of the sacrament of Marriage?

The essential characteristics of the sacrament of Marriage are unity, indissolubility and openness to the gift of children *(see n. 362)*.

## 218. What practices are contrary to Marriage?

Polygamy, adultery, divorce and lack of openness to children are among practices that contradict the nature of Marriage. Polygamy is incompatible with the unity of Marriage; adultery is an injustice to the other spouse as well as to any children of the marriage; divorce contradicts the indissolubility of Marriage by breaking apart what God has joined together in unity; and the refusal to remain open to children deprives married life of its most precious gift.

## 219. Is it ever lawful for the divorced to remarry?

Unless a Marriage has been declared null by the Church, the remarriage of the divorced while the previous partner is still alive contravenes God's plan and the law of God taught by Christ. Those who are in this situation are not to consider themselves as separated from the Church, for as baptised persons they can, and indeed must, share in her life. However, the Church reaffirms her practice of not admitting to Holy Communion divorced persons who have remarried. The Church is to pray for them, encourage them and show herself a merciful mother, and thus sustain them in faith and hope *(cf. Familiaris Consortio, § 84) (see n. 366).*

**220. What is meant by the nullity of Marriage?**
There are circumstances in which the Church may declare a Marriage to have been null and void from the beginning. This can be either because for some reason the consent exchanged by the two partners was inadequate, or because there was an impediment to their Marriage. In reaching a judgement, a Church tribunal follows a well-defined process.

**221. Why does the Church pay so much attention to Marriage and the family?**
The Christian home is the place where children first receive the faith. So the family is therefore rightly called "the Domestic Church". It should be a community of grace and prayer, and the school of human virtue and Christian love. The salvation of individuals and of human and Christian society is directly related to the happiness of the married and of the family community *(see n. 417).*

## OTHER LITURGICAL CELEBRATIONS

### 222. What are sacramentals?

Sacramentals are sacred signs instituted by the Church. They prepare people to receive the fruits of the sacraments and sanctify various aspects of human life.

### 223. What are the principal sacramentals?

Among sacramentals, blessings are especially important. These include the praise of God through his works and gifts and the intercession of the whole Church, in order that we can use God's gifts in the spirit of the Gospel.

### 224. What guidance can be given in respect of popular piety?

The Christian life is nourished first by the liturgy, but also by various kinds of popular piety rooted in different cultures. Guided by the light of faith, the Church recommends certain forms of popular piety which lead to an enrichment of the Christian life (for example, pilgrimages, the *Stations of the Cross*, the *Rosary*).

### 225. What is the purpose of a Christian funeral?

The purpose of a Christian funeral is to pray for the eternal rest of the one who has died, and also for those who mourn. At the same time it is an expression of the faith of the Christian community in eternal life.

The Crucifixion, carving, c. 420 AD (ivory). British Museum, London.

# PART THREE
# ఊ LIFE IN CHRIST ఊ

## LIFE IN CHRIST: PART 3, §§ 1691-2557

### The Human Calling: Life in the Spirit: Section 1, §§ 1691-2051

• Our vocation to blessedness: Chapter 1, §§ 1699-1876.

• The human community: Chapter 2, §§ 1877-1948.

• God's salvation: law and grace: Chapter 3, §§ 1949-2051.

### The Ten Commandments: Section 2, §§ 2052-2557

• "You shall love the Lord your God...", Chapter 1, §§ 2082-2195.

• "You shall love your neighbour as yourself", Chapter 2, §§ 2196-2557.

# THE HUMAN CALLING:
## &bull; LIFE IN THE SPIRIT &bull;

## THE DIGNITY OF THE HUMAN PERSON

### IN THE IMAGE OF GOD

### 226. What is our calling?

Made in the image and likeness of God, the human person possesses a spiritual soul, intellect and free will, and is thus destined for God and for eternal blessedness. Every person searches for perfection by seeking out and loving the true and the good.

### 227. How do we know our true human calling?

We know our true human calling through Christ, who fully discloses humankind to itself and unfolds its noble calling by revealing the mystery of the Father and the Father's love.

### 228. What should guide our behaviour?

In virtue of our calling we are bound to follow the moral law that encourages us to do good and avoid evil. This law finds an echo in our conscience.

### 229. Does our freedom incline us equally to good and to evil?

All of us have been wounded in our nature by original sin. In exercising our freedom we are thus subject to error and inclined to evil (see n. 39).

**230. How is this tendency overcome?**

Through his passion, Christ freed us from Satan and from sin. He won for us new life in the Spirit. His grace restores what sin has spoiled *(see n. 40)*.

**231. How can we develop our moral life to the full?**

The moral life grows and develops in us by grace, which enables us to follow the example of Christ. It is completed in the glory of heaven, when blessedness is fully and finally attained *(see n. 128)*.

OUR VOCATION TO BLESSEDNESS

**232. What are the Beatitudes?**

Jesus taught the Beatitudes as part of what is known as the Sermon on the Mount:

Blessed are the poor in spirit;
theirs is the kingdom of heaven.
Blessed are the gentle:
they shall have the earth for their heritage.
Blessed are those who mourn:
they shall be comforted.
Blessed are those who hunger and thirst for what is
right: they shall be satisfied.
Blessed are the merciful:
they shall have mercy shown them.

Blessed are the pure in heart: they shall see God.
Blessed are the peacemakers:
they shall be called sons of God.
Blessed are those who are persecuted in the cause
of right: theirs is the kingdom of heaven.
Blessed are you when people abuse you and persecute
you and speak all kinds of calumny against
you on my account.
Rejoice and be glad, for your reward will be great
in heaven; this is how they persecuted the prophets
before you. *(Mt 5:3-12.)*

### 233. What do the Beatitudes teach us?

The Beatitudes teach us how to face decisive choices
in our lives. By purifying our hearts, they help us to
love God above all, and to discern how best to use the
things of this world in conformity with God's law.

### 234. Do the Beatitudes show us how to reach heaven?

The Beatitudes show that God calls us to the
Kingdom of God, the vision of God, sharing in the
divine nature, eternal life, being children of God,
being at rest with God.

### 235. Can the blessedness of eternal life be achieved by our own power?

The blessedness of eternal life is beyond all our
understanding and power. It is an entirely free gift of God.

HUMAN FREEDOM

## 236. What is freedom?

Freedom is the power, rooted in reason and will, to act or not to act, to do this or that, and so to perform deliberate actions of one's own. We achieve perfection through our actions when they are directed towards God, the supreme Good.

## 237. Why has God made us free?

God has left us "free to make [our] own decisions" *(Si 15:14)* because in this way we can, of our own accord, seek our Creator, and so find a full and blessed perfection.

## 238. How should we behave so as to be free?

To act freely is to do what is good and just. The choice to do evil is an abuse of freedom and leads to the slavery of sin.

## 239. What factors may diminish personal responsibility?

Responsibility and culpability for actions may be lessened or cancelled through ignorance, violence, fear and other psychological and social factors.

## 240. Have we the right to exercise freedom?

The right to exercise freedom is necessarily part of human dignity, specifically in relation to religion and morality. However, exercising freedom does not imply the right to say or do whatever one wants, both because others' rights may be affected and because one may be mistaken.

## 241. Who can give us true freedom?

Jesus alone can give us true freedom. As Paul says: "When Christ freed us, he meant us to remain free" *(Ga 5:1)*.

### THE MORALITY OF HUMAN ACTS

## 242. On what does the morality of human acts depend?

The morality of human acts depends on the object (what is done), the end (the purpose) and the circumstances of the action. These are called the "sources" of morality.

## 243. In what way does the object make the act of the will either good or evil?

The object chosen determines the morality of the act of the will in so far as reason recognises it and judges it to be either good or evil.

### 244. Is it permissible to do something wrong so as to achieve a good end?

The end does not justify the means. It is not lawful to do evil in order to achieve something good.

### 245. What determines if an act is morally good?

An act is morally good if the object, end and circumstances are all of them good.

THE MORALITY OF THE PASSIONS

### 246. What are the passions?

The passions are emotions and feelings. The main passions are love, hate, desire, fear, joy, sadness and anger.

### 247. Are passions good or evil?

Passions, understood as movements of the senses, are in themselves neither morally good nor morally evil. However, insofar as they involve either reason or will, they do have a moral content. They can be strengthened by virtue or perverted by vice.

### 248. Does moral good require that the passions should be eliminated?

Human passions are an essential part of being human. Moral good is achieved not simply through the power of the will, but also through the heart, with all its feelings and emotions.

CONSCIENCE

### 249. What is conscience?

Conscience is a judgement of reason by which someone recognises the moral quality of a specific act. Conscience is a person's most secret core and sanctuary. There, one is alone with God, whose voice echoes deeply within.

### 250. Should conscience be educated?

Conscience must be educated and formed. A well-formed conscience is upright and truthful. It makes its judgements according to reason, in conformity with the true good willed by the wisdom of the Creator.

### 251. On what basis should conscience act?

Faced with a moral choice, conscience can make either a right judgement in accordance with reason and the divine law, or a false judgement that departs from them.

### 252. Must one always obey conscience?

One must never go against the certain judgement of conscience. Nonetheless, conscience can be ignorant or ill-informed, and can make false judgements. Such ignorance and error are not always free from guilt. It follows that we have a duty to correct and form conscience.

## 253. How can conscience be formed?

The Word of God is a light for our path. Conscience is best formed when we assimilate God's Word in faith and prayer, under the guidance of the Church's teaching, examine the situation we are in, and so discern how we should act.

VIRTUE

## 254. What are virtues?

Virtues are firm attitudes and stable dispositions that guide us to achieve the good. More precisely, they are permanent dispositions of the intellect and the will, which regulate our acts, control our passions, and direct our conduct in accordance with reason and faith. They can be grouped around the four cardinal virtues: prudence, justice, fortitude and temperance.

## 255. What is prudence?

Prudence is the virtue that assists the practical reason to discern, in any situation, the true good, and to choose the appropriate means to attain it.

## 256. What is justice?

Justice is the virtue that consists in the constant and firm will to give whatever is due to God and to one's neighbour.

### 257. What is fortitude?
Fortitude is the virtue that ensures strength in times of difficulty, and constancy in the pursuit of good.

### 258. What is temperance?
Temperance is the virtue that moderates the attraction of sensual pleasure, and teaches a balance in the use of created goods.

### 259. How can we grow in moral virtue?
We grow in moral virtue through education, by our choosing to act in certain ways, by our perseverance in times of trial, and especially by prayer. God's grace is always at work in such growth.

### 260. What other virtues are there?
Apart from moral virtues, there are the theological virtues of faith, hope and charity. These dispose Christians to live in relationship with the Blessed Trinity. They have God as their origin, motive and object. God is known through faith; he is the object of hope; he is loved in himself. These virtues are the basis of and give life to all the moral virtues.

### 261. How does faith work in us?
By faith, we believe in God and in all that he has revealed to us through the teaching and tradition of the Church *(see n. 12)*.

**262. How does hope work in us?**
Hope, allied to a firm faith, enables us to desire and wait for God, eternal life and the grace to deserve this.

**263. How does charity work in us?**
By charity, we love God above all things, and our neighbour as ourselves for God's sake. Charity "binds everything together in perfect harmony" *(Col 3:14)* and is the basis of all virtue.

**264. What are the seven gifts of the Holy Spirit?**
The seven gifts of the Holy Spirit given to Christians are wisdom, understanding, right judgement, courage, knowledge, reverence and fear of the Lord.

**265. What are the fruits of the Holy Spirit?**
The fruits of the Holy Spirit are perfections formed in us by the Spirit. Scripture lists a number of these: "Love, joy, peace, patience, kindness, goodness, trustfullness, gentleness and self control" *(Ga 5:22-23)*. There is no limit to the number of such fruits.

SIN

**266. What is sin?**
Sin is a word, action or desire contrary to the eternal law. It is an offence against God, an act of disobedience; it is in contrast with Christ's own perfect obedience.

## 267. Does sin harm human nature?

Sin is an act against reason. It wounds human nature and harms human solidarity.

## 268. Where is the root of all sin?

The root of all sin lies in the human heart.

## 269 What different kinds of sin are there?

Sins are mortal (or grave), and venial (or less serious).

## 270. When is a sin mortal?

To choose deliberately - that is, knowingly and willingly - something gravely contrary to the divine law and to the human person's final end, is to commit a mortal sin.

## 271. What are the consequences of mortal sin?

Mortal sin results in the loss of sanctifying grace, exclusion from the Kingdom of God, and the eternal death of hell *(see n. 131)*.

## 272. How can the effects of mortal sin be overcome?

Because mortal sin destroys charity in the heart, God must take the first step to overcome its immediate effects. There must be a conversion of heart in the sinner, who must normally receive sacramental absolution in the sacrament of Reconciliation. The after-effects of mortal sin, such as the tendency to sin again, can be gradually healed by the sacraments (especially Holy Communion), by humble prayer, by self-denial, and by the generous service of those in need *(see nn. 179 ff.)*.

### 273. When is a sin venial?

Someone commits a venial sin when, in a less serious matter, the moral law is not observed, or when, in a grave matter, the act is committed without full knowledge or full consent *(see n. 263)*.

### 274. How can the effects of venial sins be overcome?

The effects of venial sins can be overcome by the charity that, in spite of our sins, still remains in us.

### 275. What follows if sins are repeated?

The repetition of sins, even of venial sins, can lead to the growth of vice.

## THE HUMAN COMMUNITY

### THE INDIVIDUAL AND SOCIETY

### 276. Does the human person need society?

In order to develop according to our true nature (that is, in the image of God, One and Three), the individual needs to live in society. Certain societies, such as the family and the civil community, correspond more directly to human nature.

## 277. What is the relationship between the human person and society?

The origin, the subject and the purpose of all social institutions is and must be the human person.

## 278. What is the principle of subsidiarity?

Subsidiarity is the principle that neither the State nor any other society ought to substitute itself for the due initiative and responsibility of persons or of intermediate bodies such as the family (though, of course, it should offer such support as is required). It means taking decisions at their proper level, as close to the grass roots as is consistent with good government and the common good.

## 279. Ought society take account of moral values?

Society ought to encourage and not obstruct the exercise of virtue. It ought, moreover, to support a true hierarchy of values.

## 280. What can be done when sin pervades the social climate?

If society is suffused by sin, people must be called to a conversion of heart, and to God's grace (*cf.* the story of

Jonah). Charity is a stimulus to just reforms. There is no true solution to social questions other than the Gospel.

### SHARING IN THE LIFE OF SOCIETY

**281. Is it true that all authority comes from God?**
"You must all obey the governing authorities. Since all government comes from God, the civil authorities were appointed by God, and so anyone who resists authority is rebelling against God's decision" *(Rm 13:1-2)*.

**282. When is authority lawfully exercised in society?**
Authority is lawfully exercised when it is directed towards the common good of society. In achieving this, only morally acceptable means may be used.

**283. What is the common good?**
The common good is the totality of those social conditions that allow groups and individuals to achieve their true perfection more completely and readily.

**284. What are the essential features of the common good?**
The common good has three essential features: respect for and the promotion of the fundamental rights of the person; prosperity, or the fruitful development of the spiritual and temporal good of

society; and the peace and security of groups and of their members.

**285. Is there a duty to seek out the common good?**
The dignity of the human person requires us to seek out the common good. Everyone has the duty to uphold and sustain those institutions that try to improve the conditions of people's daily lives.

**286. Whose responsibility is it to care for the common good?**
The State has the duty to defend and promote the common good of civil society. Moreover, the common good of the whole human family requires that international society be properly organised.

SOCIAL JUSTICE

**287. In what way does society ensure social justice?**
Society ensures social justice by providing and promoting those conditions that allow groups and individuals to obtain their due rights.

**288. How is respect for the human person shown?**
Respect for the human person is shown by considering the other person as "another self". It is also shown by the respect for the fundamental rights that derive from the intrinsic dignity of the person.

### 289. Wherein lies the basis for human equality?

Equality is based on personal dignity and on those rights that flow from this.

### 290. Why do we differ one from another?

Differences between individuals belong to God's plan; he wants us to recognise our need for each other. The differences between us should encourage mutual love.

### 291. Should there be a movement towards greater equality?

The equal dignity of persons requires a commitment to the reduction of excessive social and economic inequality. It urges the elimination of sinful inequalities.

### 292. What are the characteristics of genuine solidarity?

Solidarity is an eminently Christian virtue. It is a firm and persevering determination to commit oneself to the common good; that is, to the good of all and of each individual, because we are all responsible for all. It implies a willing acceptance of others as our neighbours, for whom we must have true concern.

## GOD'S SALVATION: LAW AND GRACE

### THE MORAL LAW

### 293. What is the law?

According to Scripture, the law is God's fatherly instruction which prescribes for us the ways that lead to the promised blessedness and away from the ways of evil. It can be defined as: "A rule of conduct, enacted by competent authority, for the sake of the common good".

### 294. What is the natural law?

The natural law is a sharing in God's wisdom and goodness by each person, moulded in the image of the Creator. It expresses the dignity of the human person, and forms the basis of our fundamental rights and duties.

### 295. Is the natural law unchanging?

The natural law is unchanging and has remained unaltered throughout history. The rules that express it remain substantially valid. It provides the necessary basis for moral and civil law.

### 296. What is the Old Law?

The Old Law is the initial stage of revealed law. What it demands is summed up in the Ten Commandments. It is a preparation for the Gospel.

**297. What is the relationship between the Old Law and the natural law?**

The Old Law contains many truths naturally accessible to reason. God has revealed them because people did not read the law written in their hearts *(see n. 326)*.

**298. What is the basic characteristic of the New Law?**

The basic characteristic of the New Law is the grace of the Holy Spirit received through faith in Christ. The New Law (the Law of the Gospel) finds its main expression in the Sermon on the Mount *(Mt 5,6,7)*, and uses the sacraments to communicate grace to us *(see nn. 136 ff., 306)*.

**299. What is the relationship between the New Law and the Old Law?**

The Law of the Gospel fulfils, surpasses and perfects the Old Law. The promises of the Old Law are perfected by the Beatitudes of the Kingdom of Heaven; and its commandments are perfected by reforming the heart, the root of our actions.

**300. What are the essential features of the New Law?**

The New Law is a law of love, a law of grace, and a law of freedom.

**301. What are the evangelical counsels?**

The New Law includes the evangelical counsels. "The Church's holiness is also nourished in a special way by the many counsels whose observance the Lord commends to his disciples in the Gospel" *(Vat II: LG 42)*, in particular the call to poverty, chastity and obedience *(cf. Mt 19)*.

GRACE AND JUSTIFICATION

**302. What does the grace of the Holy Spirit confer?**

The grace of the Holy Spirit confers God's justice (or righteousness) on us. Uniting us by faith and Baptism to Christ's passion and resurrection, the Spirit makes us sharers in his life.

**303. What is justification?**

Justification is the passage from sin to the state of grace, through which the sinner becomes reconciled to God.

**304. What does justification mean?**

Like conversion, justification has two aspects: prompted by grace, people turn towards God and away from sin. Thus they accept the Lord's pardon and justice. Justification is not only the forgiveness of sin, but also the sanctification and renewal of the individual's interior being *(see n. 184)*.

### 305. Why is justification such a precious gift?

Justification has been merited for us by Christ's Passion. It is granted to us through Baptism. It conforms us to God's justice, which justifies us (makes us righteous). Its goal is the glory of God and of Christ, and the gift of eternal life. It is the most wonderful work of God's mercy.

### 306. What is grace?

God's grace is the free and undeserved help he gives us to respond to the call to become his adopted children. It draws us into the intimacy of Trinitarian life, so that we may share the divine nature and eternal life.

### 307. What is the relationship between grace and freedom?

The divine initiative in the work of grace precedes, prepares and evokes our free response. Grace responds to the deep aspirations of human freedom; it calls us to co-operate with it and to perfect it.

### 308. What is sanctifying grace?

Sanctifying (or habitual) grace is God's free gift to us of his life, poured out to us by the Holy Spirit to heal us from sin and to sanctify us. It makes us pleasing to God.

### 309. What are charisms?

Charisms are special graces of the Holy Spirit related to sanctifying grace and directed towards the common good of the Church.

### 310. What are actual graces?

Actual graces are divine actions by which God initiates and carries forward the work of our sanctification.

### 311. Is it possible to have merit in God's sight?

We have no merit before God except as a result of God's free plan to allow us to share his work of grace. Merit belongs first to God's grace, and only then depends on our collaboration. Our merit depends on the action of the Holy Spirit and on love.

### 312. Can the grace of initial conversion be merited?

No one can merit grace initially, at the beginning of the process of conversion. However, under the action of the Holy Spirit, we can subsequently merit for ourselves and for others all the graces needed to attain eternal life *(see n. 183)*.

### 313. What is Christian holiness?

Christian holiness consists essentially in the perfection of love.

### 314. Who is called to sanctity?

All the faithful, of whatever position or state of life, are called to sanctity, that is, to the fullness of the Christian life and to the perfection of love. "Christian perfection has only one limit: that of having none" *(St Gregory of Nyssa)*.

### 315. What is the road to sanctity?

The road to sanctity is through the cross: "If any want to become my followers, let them deny themselves and take up their cross and follow me" *(Mt 16:24).*

THE CHURCH, MOTHER AND TEACHER

### 316. Is there a link between the liturgy and morality?

The moral life is itself an act of worship. All Christian activity finds its nourishment in the liturgy and in the celebration of the sacraments.

### 317. What do the precepts of the Church concern?

The precepts of the Church concern the moral and Christian life united with the liturgy and nourished by it.

### 318. What are the main precepts of the Church?

The main precepts of the Church are the following:

**(1)** to take part in the celebration of Mass on Sundays and on other specified feasts;

**(2)** to confess one's grave sins at least once a year *(cf. CIC can 989)*;

**(3)** to receive Holy Communion at least during the Easter season;

**(4)** to sanctify the Holy Days as laid down by the Church;

**(5)** to observe the prescribed days of fasting and abstinence;

**(6)** to observe the marriage laws of the Church;

**(7)** to contribute to the material needs of the Church.

### 319. Should the Church's Magisterium be involved in questions of morality?

The Magisterium is the teaching authority of the Church. In moral matters, this authority is exercised by the Church's pastors in their catechesis and preaching. Their preaching is based on the Decalogue (the Ten Commandments), which expresses principles of the moral life valid for all humanity.

### 320. Can the Pope and the bishops give directives about moral matters?

It is the responsibility of the Pope and the bishops, as authoritative teachers, to preach to God's people the faith to be believed and applied in the field of morals. They also have the duty to pronounce on moral questions that fall within the natural law and reason.

### 321. Does the infallibility of the Magisterium extend to moral matters?

The infallibility of the Magisterium of the Church's pastors extends to all aspects of doctrine, including morality, without which the saving truths of the faith cannot be safeguarded, explained or observed.

# - ❧ THE TEN COMMANDMENTS ❧ -

## 322. What are the Ten Commandments?

(1) I am the Lord your God: you shall not have strange gods before me.

(2) You shall not take the name of God in vain.

(3) Remember to keep the sabbath day holy.

(4) Honour your father and your mother.

(5) You shall not kill.

(6) You shall not commit adultery.

(7) You shall not steal.

(8) You shall not bear false witness.

(9) You shall not covet your neighbour's wife.

(10) You shall not covet your neighbour's goods.

## 323. What do the Ten Commandments teach us?

The Ten Commandments (also called the "Ten Words" or "Decalogue") are part of God's revelation of himself, and teach us how God wants us to live. They express the implications of belonging to God through the covenant he has made with his people.

## 324. Are the Ten Commandments true for us today?

The Ten Commandments are true for all time. Jesus said to the young man who asked what he should do to possess eternal life: "If you wish to enter into eternal life keep the commandments" *(Mt 19:16-17)*.

Faithful to Scripture and following the example of Jesus, the Tradition of the Church has always recognised the basic importance and significance of the Ten Commandments.

### 325. Are the Commandments independent one from the other?

The Decalogue presents an organic unity, in which every commandment (or "word") relates to every other one. To break any one commandment is thus to infringe the whole Law.

### 326. Does the Decalogue refer only to the covenant between God and his people, or does it also refer to the natural law?

The gift of the Decalogue is in harmony with the covenant made by God with his people. The Commandments should be understood in their full significance in the light of this covenant. However, the Decalogue also contains a privileged expression of the natural law. It is made known to us by divine revelation and by human reason *(see n. 297)*.

### 327. How do the Commandments bind us?

In their basic content, the Ten Commandments state certain grave obligations. They also concern matters of lesser weight where the obligations will be lighter.

### 328. Is it possible to keep the Commandments?

What God commands us he makes possible for us by his grace.

### 329. How did Jesus summarise the Ten Commandments?

Jesus summarised the Ten Commandments in the two precepts of love. The first is: "You shall love the Lord your God with all your heart, with all your mind, and with all your strength". The second is: "You shall love your neighbour as yourself".

**YOU SHALL LOVE THE LORD YOUR GOD WITH ALL YOUR HEART, WITH ALL YOUR MIND, WITH ALL YOUR STRENGTH**

THE FIRST COMMANDMENT:
YOU SHALL NOT HAVE STRANGE GODS BEFORE ME

### 330. What does the first commandment require of us?

The first commandment calls us to believe in God, to hope in him, and to love him above everything else. It concerns the virtue of religion.

### 331. How is the virtue of religion practised?

The virtue of religion requires us to adore God, to pray, to offer the worship that belongs to him, and to keep the promises and vows made to him.

### 332. Does the duty to worship God apply to us only as individuals?

The duty to worship God applies to us both as individuals and as members of society. In this way we can freely profess our religion both in private and in public.

### 333. What is superstition?

Superstition is a deviation from the worship we should give to the true God. It shows itself in idolatry, as well as in various kinds of divination and magic.

### 334. What other sins are there contrary to the first commandment?

Sins against the first commandment include tempting God (putting his power to the test by word or deed), sacrilege (profaning what is consecrated to God), and simony (attempting to buy something sacred). Atheism is also a sin against this commandment since it denies the existence of God.

### 335. Is the veneration of sacred images against the first commandment?

The veneration of sacred images does not contradict the first commandment. This commandment forbids idolatry, which is giving to an image the honour due to God alone. Jesus Christ is "the image of the unseen God" *(Col 1:15)*; an image of Christ may lead us to God himself. The honour paid to sacred images is "respectful veneration", not the adoration due to God alone.

### THE SECOND COMMANDMENT:
### YOU SHALL NOT TAKE THE NAME OF GOD IN VAIN

**336. What is required by the second commandment?**
The second commandment requires us to respect the Lord's name, because the name of the Lord is holy *(see n. 442)*.

**337. What is forbidden by the second commandment?**
The second commandment forbids every improper use of God's name, and especially blasphemy. Blasphemy is the use of the name of God, of Jesus Christ, of the Virgin Mary, and of the saints in an offensive way. False oaths that call on God to be witness to a lie are also forbidden, as is perjury *(see n. 442)*.

**338. How do Christians keep God's name in mind?**
Christians keep God's name in mind in a variety of ways, and especially by prayer. They begin prayer and other activities with the sign of the cross: "In the name of the Father and of the Son and of the Holy Spirit", as a reminder of God's name and of his continual presence with us.

THE THIRD COMMANDMENT:

REMEMBER TO KEEP THE SABBATH DAY HOLY

## 339. What are the days of obligation in the Church's calendar?

Sunday is the foremost day of obligation in the Church. Other holy days of obligation vary from country to country, but will be drawn from the following: Christmas Day, the Epiphany, the Ascension, the Body and Blood of Christ, Mary the Mother of God, the Immaculate Conception, the Assumption, St Joseph, the Apostles Peter and Paul, St Patrick and All Saints *(see n. 143)*.

## 340. How should these days be made holy?

On Sundays and on other holy days of obligation the faithful are bound to take part in the celebration of Mass. They should also abstain from activities that would prevent them from giving due worship to God, from experiencing the joy proper to the Lord's Day, or from proper relaxation of mind and body *(see n. 318)*.

## 341. Has Sunday any significance for society?

The institution of Sunday is valuable for society because it helps to ensure that everyone can enjoy sufficient rest and leisure for family, cultural, social and religious activities. We should not make unnecessary demands on others that would hinder them from observing the Lord's Day.

### YOU SHALL LOVE YOUR NEIGHBOUR AS YOURSELF

THE FOURTH COMMANDMENT:
HONOUR YOUR FATHER AND MOTHER

### 342. What is the meaning of this commandment?

The fourth commandment means that, after God, we should honour our parents and those in whom, for our good, he has vested authority.

### 343. What is a family?

A man and a woman united in marriage, together with their children, form a family. The family is the domestic Church, and is the original cell of social life.

### 344. What duties do children have towards their parents?

Children owe their parents respect, gratitude, just obedience and assistance. Filial respect fosters harmony in family life.

### 345. What duties do parents have towards their children?

The first responsibility parents have towards their children is their education in faith, in prayer and in all the virtues. They have the duty to provide as best they can for the physical and spiritual needs of their children.

### 346. What are the duties of civil authorities?

Civil authorities, while being properly concerned for the good of the whole community, must respect the fundamental rights of individuals and secure the due conditions for the exercise of their freedom.

### 347. What are the duties of citizens?

It is the duty of citizens to work with the civil authorities in building up society in a spirit of truth, justice, solidarity and freedom.

### 348. Must citizens obey the law in all circumstances?

We are obliged in conscience to obey all just law. However, conscience demands that we may not follow the requirements of civil authority when such requirements are opposed to the demands of morality: "We must obey God rather than men" *(Ac 5:29)*.

### 349. Can civil society ignore the Gospel?

Every society's judgements and conduct reflect a vision of humanity and of humanity's destiny. Without the light that the Gospel sheds on God and humankind, societies can easily become totalitarian.

THE FIFTH COMMANDMENT: YOU SHALL NOT KILL

## 350. Why is it forbidden to kill?

It is forbidden to kill because every human life, from conception until death, is sacred. The human person has been made for his or her own sake in the image and likeness of the living and holy God. The murder of a human being is gravely contrary to the rights of the person and the holiness of the Creator.

## 351. Is personal defence lawful?

The prohibition of murder does not take away the right to prevent an unjust aggressor from inflicting harm. Legitimate self-defence is a grave duty for whoever is responsible for the lives of others or the common good.

## 352. What of abortion?

From conception, the child has the right to life. Direct abortion (that is, abortion willed as an end or as a means), is a shameful practice that is gravely contrary to the moral law. The Church imposes the canonical penalty of excommunication for this crime against human life.

## 353. How should the human embryo be treated?

The human embryo must be treated as a human person from conception. It must, therefore, be defended in its integrity, cared for and healed like every other human being.

### 354. What of euthanasia?

Intentional euthanasia consists in putting an end to the life of an innocent person either by act or by omission. Whatever form it takes, or whatever its motive, it is murder. It is gravely contrary to the rights and dignity of the human person and to respect for the living God, the Creator.

### 355. What of suicide?

Suicide is gravely contrary to justice, hope and charity. It is forbidden by the fifth commandment.

### 356. What is scandal?

Scandal is an attitude or behaviour that induces another to do evil. It may even lead to the other's spiritual death. It is gravely sinful if it deliberately leads others to grave sin.

### 357. What attitude ought one to have to war?

Because of the evils and injustices that all war brings with it, we must do everything reasonably possible to avoid it. The Church prays: "From famine, pestilence and war, O Lord, deliver us".

## 358. Does the moral law still stand during time of war?

The Church and human reason assert the permanent validity of the moral law during armed conflicts. Practices deliberately contrary to the law of nations and to its universal principles are crimes.

## 359. What of the arms race?

The arms race is one of the greatest curses on the human race and the harm it inflicts on the poor is more than can be endured.

THE SIXTH COMMANDMENT:
YOU SHALL NOT COMMIT ADULTERY

## 360. What is the virtue of chastity?

The virtue of chastity describes how people should show their love for each other, and how a person's sexuality finds harmony within their life as a whole. Chastity seeks to prevent someone being governed simply by impulses, desires and temptations, and chooses, through the help of God's grace, to express sexuality in ways that are genuinely good. It is a way of loving that grows and develops throughout life.

### 361. What are the principal sins gravely contrary to chastity?

The principal sins gravely contrary to chastity are seeking solitary sexual pleasure, premarital or extramarital sex, homosexual practices, and pornography.

### 362. What does the free covenant contracted between husband and wife imply?

The free covenant between husband and wife implies the indissolubility of marriage, fidelity, and openness to children.

### 363. How should the fruitfulness of marriage be understood?

Fruitfulness is a good, a gift and one of the purposes of marriage. By giving life, husband and wife share in God's fatherhood. In many places in the Bible "God's love is presented as the 'masculine' love of the bridegroom and father, but also sometimes as the 'feminine' love of a mother". The bringing forth of the Son from the Father, however, "has neither 'masculine' nor 'feminine' qualities" *(Mulieris Dignitatem, 8)*.

### 364. Is the regulation of birth lawful?

The regulation of birth is an important aspect of responsible parenthood. However, this lawful intention of husband and wife does not justify recourse to morally unacceptable means, such as contraception and sterilisation.

### 365. How may birth be lawfully regulated?

It is lawful to regulate birth by practising continence and by using the infertile period.

### 366. What are the principal offences against the dignity of marriage?

The principal offences against the dignity of marriage are adultery, divorce, polygamy and promiscuity.

### 367. What of homosexuality?

The Church has always taught that homosexual acts are wrong, because they are not open to the gift of life. Like all other people, homosexual persons are called to chastity, and to the self-mastery that leads to inner freedom. This demands the support of disinterested friendship, prayer and sacramental grace.

THE SEVENTH COMMANDMENT: YOU SHALL NOT STEAL

### 368. What is required by the seventh commandment?

The seventh commandment enjoins the practice of justice and charity in the administration of the goods of the earth and of the fruits of human work.

## 369. To whom do the goods of creation belong?

The goods of creation are destined for the whole of humanity. The right to private property does not supersede the universal goal of these goods.

## 370. What does the seventh commandment forbid?

The seventh commandment forbids stealing, that is, the taking of another's goods against the reasonable will of the owner. Every kind of taking and using another's property unjustly is against the seventh commandment. Such injustice calls for reparation. Commutative justice requires the restitution of stolen goods.

## 371. What can be said about slavery?

The moral law forbids any acts that lead to the enslavement of human beings, or to their being bought, sold or exchanged like merchandise.

## 372. Do we have absolute dominion over nature?

The dominion granted by the Creator over the mineral, vegetable and animal resources of the universe cannot be separated from moral obligations, including those towards generations yet to come.

## 373. How should we treat animals?

Animals are entrusted to our stewardship and we must show them due kindness. They may be used to serve the just satisfaction of our needs.

### 374. Is the Church concerned about economic and social problems?

The Church makes judgements about economic and social matters when the basic rights of the person or the salvation of souls require it. She is concerned with the temporal common good of all because these rights are ordered to the sovereign Good, their ultimate end.

### 375. What is the relationship between the individual and the economy?

All economic and social life is focused on the human person. The central point of social justice is that goods created by God for everyone should in fact reach everyone, in accordance with justice and with the help of charity.

### 376. What is the basic value of work?

The basic value of work stems from the human person, its author and beneficiary. By means of our work we share in the work of creation. Work united to Christ can be redemptive.

### 377. What is meant by development?

True development concerns the whole person. It is concerned with increasing each person's ability to respond to his or her vocation and hence to God's call.

## 378. What is the value and meaning of almsgiving?

Giving alms to the poor is a witness to fraternal charity: it is also a work of justice pleasing to God.

## 379. What should our attitude be to the poor?

Lazarus, the hungry beggar in the parable *(cf. Lk 17:19-31)*, should be seen in the countless people without bread, a roof or a place to stay. Jesus says to us: "As you did it not to one of the least of these, you did it not to me" *(Mt 25:45)*.

THE EIGHTH COMMANDMENT:
YOU SHALL NOT BEAR FALSE WITNESS

## 380. In what does the virtue of truth consist?

Truth or truthfulness is the virtue that consists in showing oneself true in deeds and truthful in words, and guarding against duplicity, dissimulation and hypocrisy.

## 381. What witness should the Christian give?

The Christian is not to "be ashamed of testifying to our Lord" *(2 Tm 1:8)* in word and in deed. Martyrdom is the supreme witness given to the truth of the faith.

### 382. What are the principal sins against the eighth commandment?

The principal sins against the eighth commandment are lying, perjury, detraction, calumny and rash judgement.

### 383. What is lying?

Lying consists in saying what is false with the intention of deceiving the one who has the right to the truth. If it does not cause serious damage to our neighbour it is a venial sin. Perjury is lying while under oath to tell the truth. It is gravely sinful because it dishonours the name of God who is Truth itself and who by his very nature is incapable of deceit. When committed in a court of law, perjury can contribute to the condemnation of the innocent, to the exoneration of the guilty, and to increased punishment of the accused. It thus gravely compromises the exercise of justice and fairness of judicial decisions.

### 384. What is detraction?

Detraction is revealing, without a just reason, the faults and failings of others, to those who are ignorant of them.

### 385. What is calumny?

Calumny is saying something untrue about another that harms that person's reputation.

### 386. What is rash judgement?

Rash judgement is assuming someone's guilt without sufficient reason.

**387. Ought we to keep secrets?**

The seal of the confessional is inviolable. Professional secrets must be kept. Confidences prejudicial to another must not be disclosed, save in certain exceptional circumstances (for example, relating to a criminal act).

**388. What are the rights of society in the matter of information?**

Society has the right to information based on truth, freedom and justice. One should practise moderation and discipline in the use of the social communications media.

**389. What should be done when a fault against truth is committed?**

When a fault against truth is committed, reparation must be made.

**390. Does the Church encourage the arts?**

The fine arts, especially sacred art, are directed towards expressing in some way the infinite beauty of God in works made by human hands. Their dedication to the increase of God's praise and glory is more complete, the more they are devoted to turning our minds devoutly to God.

THE NINTH COMMANDMENT:
YOU SHALL NOT COVET YOUR NEIGHBOUR'S WIFE

**391. What does the ninth commandment require?**
The ninth commandment warns against lust and concupiscence.

**392. How may one struggle against concupiscence?**
The struggle against concupiscence is achieved by purification of the heart and the practice of temperance.

**393. Why is purity of heart important?**
Purity of heart will enable us to see God: it enables us even now to see things, as it were, with God's eyes.

**394. How may one arrive at purity of heart?**
One arrives at purity of heart by prayer, the practice of chastity, probity of intention and purity of vision.

**395. What other matters are related to the ninth commandment?**
Of particular importance is modesty, which consists in the refusal to show what should remain covered. Part of this is the choice of clothing. Patience, decency and discretion also relate to modesty. Modesty is the intimate guardian of the person *(see n. 356).*

THE TENTH COMMANDMENT:
YOU SHALL NOT COVET YOUR NEIGHBOUR'S GOODS

### 396. What is prohibited by the tenth commandment?

The tenth commandment prohibits avarice and greed arising from a passion for riches and their attendant power.

### 397. What is envy?

Envy is sadness at the sight of another's goods and the immoderate desire to have them for oneself.

### 398. How can we combat envy?

We can combat envy by kindness, humility and abandonment to Divine Providence.

### 399. Is it necessary to detach oneself from riches?

Detachment from riches is essential in order to enter the Kingdom of heaven: "Blessed are the poor in spirit" *(Mt 5:3)*.

### 400. What ought to be our true desire?

"I want to see God" expresses the truest and deepest desire of the human person. Thirst for God is satisfied by the water of eternal life.

# PART FOUR
## ❧ CHRISTIAN PRAYER ❧

### CHRISTIAN PRAYER: PART 4, §§ 2558-2865

### Prayer in Daily Life: Section 1, §§ 2558 - 2758

• The revelation of prayer: Chapter 1, §§ 2566 - 2649.

• The tradition of prayer: Chapter 2, §§ 2650-2696.

• The life of prayer: Chapter 3, §§ 2697-2758.

### The Lord's prayer: Section 2, §§ 2759-2865

Tympanum depicting the family of the bishop Theotecnus, 5th- 6th century AD (mosaic). Catacombs of San Gennaro, Naples, Italy.

# ❧ PRAYER IN DAILY LIFE ❧

## THE REVELATION OF PRAYER

### 401. What is prayer?

Prayer is the raising of the mind and heart to God.

### 402. Does God want us to pray?

God tirelessly calls each of us to this mysterious encounter with himself. Prayer unfolds throughout the whole history of salvation as a reciprocal call between God and human beings.

### 403. What does the Old Testament teach us about prayer?

The Old Testament gives us the example of great men and women of prayer: like Abraham, Jacob, Moses, David, Esther, Ruth, Hannah and the prophets. The Old Testament also contains many prayers, and in particular the book of Psalms.

### 404. What is the importance of the Psalms?

The Psalms are the summit of prayer in the Old Testament. They contain two inseparable elements: personal and communal. They extend to all dimensions of history, recalling God's promises already fulfilled, and looking towards the coming of the Messiah.

**405. Are the Psalms of value today?**
The Psalms are fulfilled in Christ, who prayed them daily himself. They are an essential part of the Church's daily prayer. They are suitable for people of all ages and in every kind of society.

**406. What does the New Testament teach us about prayer?**
Jesus often prayed to his Father alone and in silence. He gives us a perfect model of prayer. His prayer shows his loving adherence to his Father's will, especially in accepting the cross. He had absolute confidence that he would always be heard.

**407. What should be the qualities of prayer according to Jesus' teaching?**
Jesus teaches his disciples to pray with a purified heart, with lively and persevering faith, with filial boldness. He calls them to vigilance and invites them to present their petitions to God in his name. Jesus Christ himself listens to prayers addressed to him.

**408. What are the characteristics of Mary's prayer?**
Two great prayers of the Virgin Mary were her *Fiat* in which she said "Yes" to what God asked of her, and her prayer of praise the *Magnificat*. They are characterised by the generous offering of her whole being in faith.

**409. Who teaches us to pray?**

The Holy Spirit is the first to teach us how to pray. The Spirit instructs the Church in the life of prayer, inspiring new expressions of the same basic forms of prayer: blessing, petition, intercession, thanksgiving and praise *(see nn. 82, 93, 413)*.

**410. What are these forms of prayer in more detail?**

A traditional division of prayer is into adoration, contrition, thanksgiving and supplication. The prayer of *adoration* (or *praise*) is entirely disinterested and rises to God, praising him and giving him glory for his own sake - not for what he has done, but simply because he is. The prayer of *contrition* seeks forgiveness for sin, and the strength to avoid sin. The prayer of *thanksgiving* arises from every joy and suffering, every event and need of our lives: "Give thanks in all circumstances" *(1 Th 5:18)*. In the prayer of *supplication* (or *petition*) we ask for all we need and for the needs of others. This prayer knows no boundaries and extends even to one's enemies.

### THE TRADITION OF PRAYER

**411. What are the principal sources of prayer?**

The principal sources of prayer are the Word of God, the Liturgy of the Church, and the virtues of faith, hope and charity.

### 412. To whom is prayer directed?

Prayer is primarily addressed to God the Father. It may also be directed towards Jesus, or the Holy Spirit. Thus: "Lord Jesus Christ, Son of God, have mercy on us sinners"; "Come Holy Spirit, fill the hearts of your faithful" *(see nn. 39-42)*.

### 413. What part does the Holy Spirit play in prayer?

"No one can say, 'Jesus is Lord', without the action of the Holy Spirit" *(1 Co 12:3)*. The Church encourages us to invoke the Holy Spirit as the inner Teacher of the Christian's prayer *(see nn. 82, 93, 409)*.

### 414. Does the Blessed Virgin Mary enter into our life of prayer?

Because of Mary's unique cooperation with the action of the Holy Spirit, the Church loves to pray in communion with her, to praise with her the great things the Lord has done for her and to entrust our requests and praises to her *(see nn. 53, 114)*.

### 415. What are the principal prayers invoking Our Lady?

These are the *Hail Mary* and the *Rosary*. The mysteries of the *Rosary* are a summary of everything in the Gospel.

**416. May we also invoke the saints?**

In prayer, the pilgrim Church is associated with the prayer of the saints, whose intercession she asks. *(see n. 113)*.

**417. Where should we first learn to pray?**

The first place where most people learn to pray is within the Christian family *(see n. 221)*.

**418. How can we be helped to pray?**

Apart from the family, there are many individuals who can help us to pray: for example, the clergy, religious, and spiritual directors can guide us. By receiving catechesis, by taking part in prayer groups, as well as by belonging to lay or religious groups, we can be helped to pray.

**419. What are the most appropriate places for prayer?**

The proper place for liturgical prayer for the parish community and the privileged place for eucharistic adoration is a church. Other special places are monasteries, convents and places of pilgrimage. Nonetheless, wherever we are it is possible for us to be united to God in prayer. "When you pray, go to your private room and, when you have shut your door, pray to your Father who is in that secret place, and your Father who sees all that is done in secret will reward you" *(Mt 6:6)*.

## THE LIFE OF PRAYER

### 420. When does the Church invite us to pray?
The Church invites the faithful to regular prayer: daily prayers, the Liturgy of the Hours, Sunday Eucharist (Mass), the feasts of the liturgical year *(see n. 144)*.

### 421. What are the basic ways of praying?
There are three basic ways of praying: vocal prayer, meditation and contemplative prayer. These have in common the raising of the mind and heart to God.

### 422. What is vocal prayer?
Vocal prayer is prayer which, based on the unity of body and spirit, associates the body with the interior prayer of the heart, following Christ's example of praying to his Father, and teaching the "Our Father" to his disciples.

### 423. What is meditation?
Meditation is a prayerful quest engaging thought, imagination, emotion and will. Its aim is to make our own, in faith, the subject considered, by deepening and comparing it with the reality of our own life.

## 424. What is contemplative prayer?

Contemplative prayer is the simplest expression of the mystery of prayer. It is a gaze of faith fixed on Jesus, an attentiveness to the Word of God, a silent love. It achieves real union with the prayer of Christ to the extent that it enables us to share in his mystery.

## 425. Will prayer be easy?

We will almost always have to try hard in order to pray, because it involves a fight against ourselves and the wiles of the Tempter. The struggle to pray is part of our "spiritual battle" as we try to act according to the Spirit of Christ: we pray as we live, because we live as we pray.

## 426. What are the principal difficulties in prayer?

The principal difficulties in prayer are distraction and dryness. The remedy lies in faith, conversion and vigilance of heart.

## 427. What are the principal temptations that threaten prayer?

Temptations that threaten prayer are lack of faith, and accidie, which is a kind of depression arising from a lack of vigilance and asceticism. However, we need not be discouraged, provided we can respond with humility, confidence and perseverance. "The spirit indeed is willing, but the flesh is weak" *(Mt 26:41)*.

### 428. Does our prayer influence what happens?

Christian prayer implies co-operation with God's will, and with his plan of love for everyone.

### 429. Why does it seem that God is often slow to hear our prayer?

Our trust is put to the test when it seems that God is deaf to our prayer. God wants only what is good for us. The Lord wants our desires to be so trained through prayer that we may be able to accept what he proposes to give us.

### 430. What should we do when it seems that God does not hear our prayer?

When it seems God does not hear our prayer, the Gospel tells us to ask ourselves whether our prayer is in conformity with what the Spirit wants.

### 431. When ought we to pray?

"Pray constantly", says St Paul *(1 Th 5:17)*. It is always possible to pray. It is absolutely necessary. Prayer and the Christian life are inseparable.

## THE LORD'S PRAYER: "OUR FATHER"

### A SUMMARY OF THE WHOLE GOSPEL

**432. Did Jesus teach his disciples any particular prayer?**

Jesus taught his disciples the "Our Father":

Our Father, who art in heaven,

hallowed be thy name;

thy kingdom come;

thy will be done

on earth as it is in heaven.

Give us this day our daily bread;

and forgive us our trespasses

as we forgive those who trespass against us;

and lead us not into temptation,

but deliver us from evil.

**433. When did Jesus teach this prayer?**

He taught this prayer in response to his disciples' request: "Lord, teach us to pray" *(Lk 11:1)*. The *Our Father* is a truly perfect prayer: it is a summary of the whole Gospel; it is at the centre of the Scriptures. It is also called the *Lord's Prayer*, because it was taught by the Lord Jesus.

## 434. Does the Church regularly use this prayer?

The *Lord's Prayer* is above all others the prayer of the Church. It is an integral part of the Divine Office and of the sacraments of Christian initiation: Baptism, Confirmation and Eucharist. In the context of the Eucharist, it reveals the eschatological character of its petitions, hoping for the Lord, "until he comes" *(1 Co 11:26)*.

OUR FATHER WHO ART IN HEAVEN

## 435. What should our attitude be when we say this prayer?

When we say this prayer we should show simple and faithful trust, humble and joyous assurance. *Abba*, which we translate as 'Father', is in Jesus' own language an affectionate and intimate term for which there is no precise equivalent in English.

## 436. Why can we call on God as Father?

We can call on God as Father because the Son of God, made man, has revealed him to us. In this Son, through Baptism, we are incorporated and adopted as children of God *(see n. 148)*.

### 437. With whom does this prayer bring us into communion?

The *Lord's Prayer* brings us into communion with the Father and with his Son, Jesus Christ. At the same time, it reveals us to ourselves.

### 438. How should our praying of the *Our Father* change us?

Praying the *Our Father* should develop in us the will to become like him, and foster in us a humble and trusting heart.

### 439. What should the word "our" remind us of?

When we say "our" Father, we recall the new Covenant in Jesus Christ, through whom the Lord is our God and we are his People. We are reminded that we are members of the Church, which is a communion with the Persons of the Blessed Trinity and of us with each other *(see nn. 112, 113)*.

### 440. What does the phrase "who art in heaven" mean?

"Who art in heaven" does not refer to a place but to God's majesty and his presence in the hearts of the just. Heaven, the Father's house, is the true homeland towards which we are heading and to which even now we belong.

THE SEVEN PETITIONS

## 441. How can the different petitions in the *Our Father* be divided?

In the *Our Father*, the object of the first three petitions is the glory of the Father: the sanctification of his name, the coming of the kingdom and the fulfilment of his will. The four others present our wants to him: they ask that our lives be nourished, healed of sin, guided in right ways, and made victorious in the struggle with evil.

## 442. What is meant by the first petition: Hallowed be thy name?

God's name was revealed first to Moses and then in Jesus. When we pray "hallowed be thy name" we become part of God's plan to keep his name holy and so become holy ourselves. The holiness of God's name is seen in us and through us; and also in every nation and in every person.

## 443. What is meant by the second petition: Thy kingdom come?

By the second petition, the Church looks first to Christ's return and the final coming of God's Kingdom. It also prays for the growth of the Kingdom of God in the "today" of our own lives.

**444. What is meant by the third petition: Thy will be done?**

In the third petition, we ask the Father to unite our will to that of his Son, so as to fulfil his plan of salvation for the world.

**445. What is meant by the fourth petition: Give us this day our daily bread?**

In the fourth petition, by saying "give us", we express in communion with our fellow men and women, our filial trust in our heavenly Father. "Our daily bread" refers both to the material nourishment that everyone needs to live, and especially to the Bread of Life, which is the Word of God and the Body of Christ. It is received as the essential nourishment of the Heavenly Banquet prefigured in the Eucharist.

**446. What is meant by the fifth petition: Forgive us our trespasses?**

The fifth petition begs God's mercy for our offences, mercy that can penetrate our hearts only if, with the example and help of Christ, we have learned to forgive our enemies.

**447. What is meant by the sixth petition: Lead us not into temptation?**

When we say "lead us not into temptation" we are asking God not to let us take the path leading to sin.

This petition implores God for the Spirit of
discernment and strength; it requests the grace of
vigilance and final perseverance.

### 448. What is meant by the seventh petition: Deliver us from evil?

Christ has triumphed over Satan, the "prince of this
world". In praying "deliver us from evil", we pray
with the Church that God will reveal this victory to us
and give us a share in it *(see n. 35)*.

### 449. What is the final doxology and what does it mean?

The final doxology is: "For the kingdom, the power
and the glory are yours, now and forever". This
acclamation recapitulates the first three petitions,
knowing that the power of the Evil One is broken, and
that all kingship, power and glory have been restored
by Christ to the Father. The doxology looks forward to
the completion of salvation when God will be all in all.

### 450. What does the final "Amen" signify?

"After the prayer is over you say 'Amen', which
means 'So be it', thus ratifying with our 'Amen' what
is contained in the prayer that God has taught us' *(St
Cyril of Jerusalem)*.

# ❧ SOME DAILY PRAYERS ❧

### THE SIGN OF THE CROSS

In the name of the Father, and of the Son and of the Holy Spirit. Amen.

### THE OUR FATHER

Our Father,
who art in heaven,
hallowed be thy name;
thy kingdom come;
thy will be done on earth
as it is in heaven.
Give us this day our daily bread;
and forgive us our trespasses,
as we forgive those who trespass against us;
and lead us not into temptation,
but deliver us from evil. Amen.

### THE GLORY BE TO THE FATHER

Glory be to the Father, and to the Son, and to the Holy Spirit, as it was in the beginning, is now and ever shall be, world without end. Amen.

### A PRAYER TO THE HOLY SPIRIT

Come, O Holy Spirit, fill the hearts of your faithful, and kindle in them the fire of your love.

**V.** Send forth your Spirit, and they shall be created.

**R.** And you shall renew the face of the earth.

Let us pray

O God, who taught the hearts of the faithful, by the light of the Holy Spirit, grant, that by the gift of the same Spirit, we may be always truly wise, and ever rejoice in his consolations. We make our prayer through Christ our Lord.

**R.** Amen.

### THE HAIL MARY

Hail Mary, full of grace, the Lord is with thee. Blessed art thou amongst women, and blessed is the fruit of thy womb, Jesus. Holy Mary, Mother of God, pray for us sinners, now and at the hour of our death. Amen.

### AN ACT OF FAITH

O my God, I believe in you and in all your Church teaches, because you have said it, and your word is true.

### AN ACT OF HOPE

O my God, I hope in you, for grace and for glory, because of your promises, your mercy and your power.

### AN ACT OF LOVE

O my God, I love you above all things, and for your sake I love my neighbour as myself.

### AN ACT OF CONTRITION

O my God, because you are so good, I am very sorry that I have sinned against you, and by the help of your grace I will not sin again.

### A MORNING OFFERING

O my God, I offer you all my prayers, works, joys and sufferings of this day. Grant that they may be according to your will, and for your great glory. Keep me from all sin and evil, and may your grace be always with me, and with those I love.

### THE ANGELUS

**V.** The angel of the Lord declared unto Mary;
**R.** And she conceived by the Holy Spirit.

Hail Mary...

**V.** Behold the handmaid of the Lord;
**R.** Be it done unto me according to your word.

Hail Mary...

**V.** And the Word was made Flesh:
**R.** And dwelt among us.

Hail Mary...

**R.** Pray for us, O holy Mother of God:
**V.** That we may be made worthy of the promises of Christ.

Let us pray

Pour forth, we beseech you, O Lord, your grace into our hearts, that we, to whom the incarnation of Christ, your Son, was made known by the message of an angel, may, by his passion and cross, be brought to the glory of his resurrection, through the same Christ our Lord.
Amen.

### THE DIVINE PRAISES

Blessed be God.
Blessed be his holy Name.
Blessed be Jesus Christ, true God and true Man.
Blessed be the name of Jesus.
Blessed be his most Sacred Heart.
Blessed be his most Precious Blood.
Blessed be Jesus in the most holy Sacrament of the Altar.
Blessed be the Holy Spirit, the Paraclete.

Blessed be the great Mother of God,
Mary most holy.
Blessed be her holy and Immaculate Conception.
Blessed be her glorious Assumption.
Blessed be the name of Mary, Virgin and Mother.
Blessed be St Joseph, her spouse most chaste.
Blessed be God, in his Angels and in his Saints.

## THE MYSTERIES OF THE ROSARY

### THE JOYFUL MYSTERIES

**1.** The Annunciation.

**2.** The Visitation.

**3.** The Nativity.

**4.** The Presentation.

**5.** The Finding in the Temple.

### THE MYSTERIES OF LIGHT

**1.** The Baptism in the Jordan.

**2.** The Wedding at Cana.

**3.** The Proclamation of the Kingdom of God.

**4.** The Transfiguration.

**5.** The Institution of the Eucharist.

### THE SORROWFUL MYSTERIES

**1.** The Agony in the Garden.

**2.** The Scourging at the Pillar.

**3.** The Crowning with Thorns.

**4.** The Carrying of the Cross.

**5.** The Crucifixion.

### THE GLORIOUS MYSTERIES

**1.** The Resurrection.

**2.** The Ascension.

**3.** The Descent of the Holy Spirit.

**4.** The Assumption.

**5.** The Crowning of Our Lady in Heaven,
and the Glory of all the Saints.

### THE HAIL HOLY QUEEN (SALVE REGINA)

Hail, holy Queen, mother of mercy; hail, our life, our sweetness, and our hope! To you do we cry, poor banished children of Eve; to you do we send up our sighs, mourning and weeping in this vale of tears. Turn then, most gracious advocate, your eyes of mercy towards us; and after this our exile, show to us the blessed fruit of your womb, Jesus. O clement, O loving, O sweet Virgin Mary.

**V.** Pray for us, O holy Mother of God.
**R.** That we may be made worthy of the promises of Christ.

## THE REGINA CÆLI

O Queen of heaven, rejoice! alleluia.
For he whom you did merit to bear, alleluia.
Has risen as he said, alleluia.
Pray for us to God, alleluia.
**V.** Rejoice and be glad, O Virgin Mary, alleluia.
**R.** For the Lord has risen indeed, alleluia.

Let us pray
O God, who gave joy to the world through the resurrection of your son our Lord Jesus Christ, grant that we may obtain, through his Virgin Mother, Mary, the joys of everlasting life. Through the same Christ our Lord. Amen.

## THE MEMORARE

Remember, O most loving Virgin Mary, that it is a thing unheard of, that anyone ever had recourse to your protection, implored your help, or sought your intercession, and was left unaided. Filled, therefore, with confidence in your goodness, I fly to you, O Mother, Virgin of virgins. To you I come, before you I stand, a sorrowful sinner. Despise not my poor words, O Mother of the Word of God, but graciously hear and grant my prayer. Amen.

### THE DE PROFUNDIS

Out of the depths I cry to you, O Lord,
Lord, hear my voice!
O let your ears be attentive
to the voice of my pleading.

If you, O Lord, should mark our guilt,
Lord, who would survive?
But with you is found forgiveness:
for this we revere you.

My soul is waiting for the Lord,
I count on his word.
My soul is longing for the Lord
more than watchmen for daybreak.
Let the watchman count on daybreak
and Israel on the Lord.

Because with the Lord there is mercy
and fullness of redemption.
Israel indeed he will redeem
from all its iniquity.

**V.** Eternal rest grant unto them O Lord.
**R.** And let perpetual light shine upon them.
**V.** May they rest in peace.
**R.** Amen.

Let us pray
O God, the Creator and Redeemer of all the faithful,
grant to the souls of your servants departed the
remission of all their sins, that through our pious

supplication they may obtain that pardon which they have always desired; who lives and reigns for ever and ever. Amen.

## PRAYER BEFORE A CRUCIFIX

Behold, O kind and most sweet Jesus, I cast myself on my knees in your sight, and with the most fervent desire of my soul, I pray and beseech you that you would impress upon my heart, lively sentiments of faith, hope and charity, with a true repentance for my sins, and a firm desire of amendment; while with deep affection and grief of soul I ponder within myself and mentally contemplate your five most precious wounds; having before my eyes that which David spoke in prophecy of you, O good Jesus: "They have pierced my hands and my feet; they have numbered all my bones".

## THE ANIMA CHRISTI (SOUL OF CHRIST)

Soul of Christ, make me holy.
Body of Christ, save me.
Blood of Christ, fulfil me.
Water from the side of Christ, cleanse me.
Passion of Christ, fortify me.
O good Jesus, hear me.
Within your wounds Lord, lose me.
Never let me leave you.

From all evil, protect me.
Through death's door, beckon me,
And call me to you,
So may I join the saints in praising you,
Always and for ever.
Amen.

### SOME PRAYERS OF THE SAINTS

Teach us, good Lord,
to serve you as you deserve;
to give and not to count the cost,
to fight and not to heed the wounds,
to toil and not to seek for rest,
to labour and not to ask for any reward,
save that of knowing that we do your will.
*(St Ignatius)*

Lord, make me an instrument of your peace:
  where there is hatred, let me sow love;
  where there is injury, let me sow pardon;
  where there is doubt, let me sow faith;
  where there is despair, let me give hope;
  where there is darkness, let me give light;
  where there is sadness, let me give joy.
O Divine Master, grant that I may try
  not to be comforted, but to comfort;
  not to be understood, but to understand;
  not to be loved, but to love.

Because it is in giving that we receive,
it is in forgiving that we are forgiven,
and it is in dying that we are born to eternal life.
*(St Francis of Assisi)*

Thanks be to you, my Lord Jesus Christ,
for all the benefits which you have given me,
for all the pains and insults
which you have borne for me.
O most merciful Redeemer, Friend and Brother,
may I know you more clearly,
love you more dearly,
follow you more nearly, day by day.
*(St Richard of Chichester)*

### NIGHT PRAYER

Save us, O Lord, while we are awake, and protect us while we sleep, so that we may watch with Christ, and rest with him in peace.

Visit, we beseech you, O Lord, this house and family, and drive far from it all the snares of the enemy; let your holy Angels dwell with us, and keep us in peace; and may your blessing be always upon us.

May our Lord bless us and preserve us from all evil, and bring us to life everlasting. Amen.

And may the souls of the faithful departed through the mercy of God rest in peace. Amen.

146

# ❧ GENERAL INDEX ❧

# ❧ GLOSSARY ❧

**Absolution:** The pardon (forgiveness) granted to the sinner within the sacrament of Penance (also called Reconciliation or Confession) by the priest, through the power given to the Church by Christ. "Whose sins you shall forgive they are forgiven" *(Jn 20:23)*.

**Age of Reason:** The age of seven years, at which it is presumed the child has the use of reason and is capable of exercising personal responsibility. It is at this age that a child is permitted to receive the sacraments of Holy Communion and Reconciliation for the first time.

**Annunciation:** The visit of the Angel Gabriel to Mary to invite her to be Mother of Jesus, the Son of God, is called the Annunciation. It is described in *Luke 1:26-38*.

**Apostle:** An apostle is one who is sent out to preach the Gospel as Jesus sent the first Apostles: "Go, therefore, make disciples of all the nations; baptise them in the name of the Father and of the Son and of the Holy Spirit, and teach them to observe all the commands I gave you" *(Mt 28:18-20)*.

**Apostles' Creed:** A traditional statement of the faith of the Church deriving from the early Church of Rome, used in particular for those who were preparing for Baptism.

**Apostolate:** The work of the Christian to proclaim and extend the Kingdom of God.

**Apostolic succession:** The handing on from the apostles to their successors the bishops, the responsibility to teach and maintain the Catholic faith throughout the world.

**Ascension:** The entry of the humanity of Jesus into heaven, where he will be until the end of time. The apostles were told: "Jesus who has been taken up from you into heaven, this same Jesus will come back in the same way as you have seen him go there" *(Ac 1:11).*

**Assumption:** This is the teaching that when her earthly life was finished, Our Lady was taken up body and soul to heaven. In this way she shares very specially in her Son's resurrection; it is also an anticipation of the resurrection of other Christians.

**Baptism:** The sacrament of birth into the Christian life which leads to all the other sacraments. Along with Confirmation and the Eucharist it initiates someone into the Church, remits all sin both personal and original, and begins the new life of grace.

**Beatitude:** The blessedness or happiness of heaven, which is beyond description. "Things beyond the mind of man, all that God has prepared for those who love him" *(1 Co 2:9).*

**Beatitudes:** Teachings of Jesus in the Sermon on the Mount which show the Christian way of life and its meaning. They are a series of apparently paradoxical statements, each pointing to characteristics of true blessedness *(see Mt 5:1-12; Lk 6:20-23).*

**Blasphemy:** Thoughts, words or actions against God or against godly things. It is contrary to the second commandment.

**Catechesis:** Education in the faith of the Church. Its purpose is to lead people to communion with Christ, to build up the community of believers, and to strengthen the missionary activity of the Church. Those who give catechesis are called "catechists".

**Catechumen:** An adult who desires baptism and who enrols in a programme of preparation for baptism (the catechumenate). The catechumenate, belonging to the Rite of Christian Initiation of

Adults *(the RCIA)*, aims to bring the individual's conversion and faith to maturity within a Church community.

**Celibacy:** Remaining unmarried. Usually the term is used to describe someone who remains in this state "for the sake of the kingdom", and in particular priests and religious. All are called to chastity; not all are called to celibacy *(see chastity)*.

**Charism:** A supernatural gift bestowed by the Holy Spirit for building up the body of Christ. It is given not for personal benefit but for the common good. "There is a variety of gifts but always the same Spirit... The particular way in which the Spirit is given to each person is for a good purpose" *(see 1 Co 12:4-11)*.

**Chastity:** Chastity means the successful integration of sexuality within the person; it thus promotes the inner unity within someone's bodily and spiritual being *(see celibacy)*.

**Common Good, The:** The idea that society should be organised for the benefit of all its members. It "embraces the sum total of those conditions of social living, whereby people are enabled more fully and more readily to achieve their own perfection" *(Mater et magistra, § 65)*. It promotes unselfishness, sharing, working for the good of others.

**Contrition:** Heartfelt sorrow for and detestation of sin, with the resolve not to sin again. It is called "perfect" if it is born solely out of love for God's goodness.

**Council, Ecumenical:** An Ecumenical Council of the Church is a gathering of the bishops under the authority of the Pope, for the guidance of the whole Church.

**Covenant:** A binding agreement between two parties, in particular between God and human beings. The Old Covenant refers to the basic agreement: "You shall be my people and I will be your

God"*(Ezk 36:28)*, which is repeated in one form or another throughout the Old Testament. The New Covenant is the unique and radical fulfilment of this promise through Christ's death and resurrection, celebrated in the Eucharist *(see Lk 22:20; 1 Co 11:23-25)*.

**Diocese:** A diocese is a portion of the People of God, entrusted to the care of a bishop. It is a community of the faithful - lay and clergy - gathered round the bishop, especially for the celebration of the Eucharist.

**Ecumenism:** The movement that promotes unity among Christians, in response to Christ's prayer: "May they all be one. Father, may they be one in us, as you are in me and I am in you, so that the world may believe it was you who sent me" *(Jn 17:21)*. The principles of the ecumenical movement are based on the real but imperfect communion which joins Catholics to all who confess Jesus Christ as Lord and Saviour according to the scriptures, and share a common Baptism. *(See the Decree on Ecumenism of the Second Vatican Council.)*

**Epiphany:** The feast that commemorates the manifestation of the new-born Jesus as the Messiah, recognised by the Wise Men from the Gentile world. Usually God both manifests himself and veils himself at the same time, supremely at the Incarnation.

**Eucharist:** This is the central act of Christian worship. It is an act of praise and thanksgiving; it is prayer and celebration; it is communion in the death and resurrection of Christ (the paschal mystery). The liturgical celebration of the Eucharist is also known as the Sacrifice of the Mass. It is the final sacrament of initiation (after Baptism and Confirmation) by which a Christian is incorporated into the Church. The Eucharist also refers to the abiding presence of Christ's body and blood sacramentally under the appearance of bread and wine; as such it is usually called the Blessed Sacrament.

**Eucharistic Assembly:** A name given to the gathering of people who assemble for the celebration of Mass.

**Evangelical Counsels:** The Gospel is a call to holiness and is addressed to everyone. In the Sermon on the Mount Jesus tells his hearers that they must be perfect *(see Mt 5:48)*, in other words they must never stop trying to grow in holiness. There are many counsels in the Gospel, especially those indicated in the Beatitudes, but some people are invited to grow in holiness through following the counsels of poverty, chastity and obedience -these are known as the evangelical counsels.

**Evangelisation:** The work of proclaiming the Kingdom of God. "The Church evangelises when she seeks to convert, solely through the Divine Power of the Message she proclaims, both the personal and collective consciences of people, the activities in which they engage, and the lives and the concrete milieus which are theirs" *(Evangelii Nuntiandi, § 18)*.

**Expiation:** The act of redemption and atonement for sin that Christ won for us through his death and resurrection. The Church's faith in the saving power of Christ's death comes from its initial faith in his resurrection. "Unless a wheat grain falls on the ground and dies, it remains only a single grain; but if it dies, it yields a rich harvest. Anyone who loves his life loses it; anyone who hates his life in this world will keep it for the eternal life" *(Jn 12:24-25)*.

**Faithful, The:** People of God or the members of the Church. The majority of these are the "lay faithful" or the "laity"; others are clergy (bishops, priests, deacons); others are religious (brothers, nuns), though, strictly speaking, religious are also lay people.

**Grace:** God's free and undeserved gifts to us to help us respond to the call to become his adopted children *(see nn. 304-308)*.

**Immortality:** Not subject to death or decay. In particular it refers to the human soul, which does not die with the body, but continues to exist, waiting for the final resurrection, when body and soul will be reunited.

**Incarnation:** The doctrine that God has become man in Jesus Christ, who is truly God and truly man in the unity of one Divine Person. His coming is described: "The Word was made flesh, he lived among us" *(Jn 1:14)*.

**Infallibility:** The gift of the Holy Spirit to the Church guaranteeing that the Church will never teach error in matters of faith and morals. It is a gift exercised by the Pope as Peter's successor, and by the Pope with the bishops in union with him.

**Liturgy:** The public worship of the Church, celebrated in union with the local bishop according to the norms determined by Rome.

**Morality:** This refers to the goodness or evil of a human act. The morality of an action depends on the object, the intention and the circumstances of the action.

**Mystery of Faith:** A way of indicating the essential aspects of Christian redemption. Summarised in the various responses to the invitation during the celebration of the Eucharist: "Let us proclaim the Mystery of Faith", thus, "Christ has died, Christ is risen, Christ will come again".

**Mystery of Salvation:** The wonderful truth that God loves us and has made it possible for us to become free, to know him and to be with him. This is the Good News (the Gospel) for all people *(see Lk 2:10)*.

**Mystery:** A truth beyond our complete grasp, but which we are invited to reflect on so that we may grow in faith and in understanding. Almost all truth has within it an element of mystery, not least the truth about ourselves.

**Mystical Body:** The Mystical Body of Christ is a name given to the Church. It derives from Christ's own reference to the vine and the branches *(Jn 15:5)*, and especially from St Paul's teaching in many of his letters *(Rm 12:5; 1 Co 12; Ep 4&5; Col 1:24)*. The metaphor he uses of the Church is of a body, with Christ the head and the faithful as the members.

**Nicene Creed:** A formula of faith deriving from the first two great Councils of the Church, Nicea (325 AD) and Constantinople (381 AD). It is in common usage in all the great Churches of both East and West today. It is the Creed normally proclaimed during Sunday Mass in the Latin Rite.

**Original Sin:** Following the fall from grace of our first parents when they chose to go their own way rather than God's, they passed to their descendants a wounded human nature, susceptible to sin. This state is called "original sin".

**Paradise:** An image of how our first parents were before the Fall, when they lived in perfect friendship with God *(see Gn 2:4-24)*. It also refers to heaven, the final home of the just where they will live in perfect friendship with God.

**Parish:** A community of the faithful within a diocese under the pastoral care of a priest appointed to this pastoral responsibility by the bishop.

**Paschal Mystery:** See *Redemption*.

**Passover:** The great Jewish festival which celebrates the deliverance of the Jews from slavery in Egypt *(see Ex 12)*. The new Passover is the Eucharist, inaugurated by Jesus at the Last Supper, which brings about and celebrates the deliverance of all mankind from death to new life: "By dying he destroyed our death, by rising he restored our life".

**Praise:** The form of prayer that specifically gives honour and glory to God. St Augustine writes in the *Confessions*: "You are great, O Lord, and greatly to be praised: great is your power and your wisdom is without measure. And man, so small a part of your creation, wants to praise you... You yourself encourage him to delight in your praise, for you have made us for yourself, and our heart is restless until it rests in you."

**Prophecy:** An utterance made on God's behalf under the influence of the Holy Spirit. It is a charism referred to by St Paul *(1 Co 14)*.

**Prophet:** One who speaks on God's behalf, and in particular to lead God's people in right ways. The last and greatest of the prophets was John the Baptist, whose task it was to prepare the way for Christ and to point him out to others.

**Purgatory:** A state of purification after death for those who have died as God's friends but who are not yet ready to enter heaven.

**Redemption:** The process by which the change from slavery to freedom takes place. Everyone is in some way a slave to sin, death, the powers of the world and so on; the liberation sought is forgiveness, new birth, freedom and so on. The redemption of humanity has been brought about by Christ, our Redeemer, through his passion, death, resurrection and ascension - this is the Paschal Mystery.

**Religious:** Men and women who consecrate their whole lives to God, living out the evangelical counsels of poverty, chastity and obedience, and following a special rule of life.

**Remission of Sins:** See *Absolution*.

**Revelation:** The words and actions by which God communicates himself to his people and makes known the divine plan. The climax of revelation is the coming among us of Jesus Christ, the Incarnate Word of God. The Son is the Father's definitive Word, so there will be no further revelation after him.

**Rites:** The rich variety of liturgical traditions by which the faith is celebrated in different parts of the Church, arising out of the diverse cultures, traditions and languages of different peoples. Thus there are Latin rites in the West, and a number of Oriental rites in the East.

**Sacrament:** A sacrament is an outward sign of inward grace instituted by Jesus Christ, by which we share in the divine life. There are seven sacraments entrusted to the Church, namely Baptism, Confirmation, Eucharist, Penance, Anointing of the Sick, Holy Orders and Matrimony.

**Saint:** Someone who is judged by the Church to to be now in heaven, having lived a life of great holiness. The process by which a person is declared to be a saint is called "canonisation".

**Salvation:** The forgiveness of sin and restoration of friendship with God that comes through faith. "He who believes and is baptised will be saved, but he who does not believe will be condemned" *(Mk 16:16)*.

**Sanctification:** The process of being made holy. The work of the Church is the work of the sanctification of all people; this is the particular work of the Holy Spirit.

**Solidarity:** The principle that we are responsible for each other, willing to see others as another "self" and to see injustice to others as no less serious than injustice to oneself. It is "a firm and persevering determination to commit oneself to the common good; that is to say, to the good of all and of each individual because we are all really responsible for all" *(Sollicitudo Rei Socialis, § 38)*.

**Soul:** In Scripture the word "soul" often refers to human life or to the entire human person. However the word also signifies the spiritual principle of our being, directly created by God. Soul and body together form a unique persons *(see Immortality)*.

**Spiritual:** Relating to the spirit or soul, or to sacred things, and not to material things. "From the beginning of time God made at once out of nothing both orders of creatures, the spiritual and the corporeal, that is, the angelic and the earthly, and then the human creature, who as it were shares in both orders, being composed of spirit and body" *(Fourth Lateran Council)*.

**Subsidiarity:** The principle that authority should be exercised so that decisions are taken as close to the grass roots as is consistent with good government. It promotes the common good, and protects the rights of individuals and of smaller societies by enabling them to take part in the decision-making process.

**Suffering Servant:** A term used by Isaiah *(52-53)*. The Servant suffers and dies; his death is mysterious because of his innocence; his death is a vicarious atonement, vindicated by his resurrection. By his loving obedience to the Father, Jesus fulfils the atoning mission of the Suffering Servant, who will "justify many, taking their faults on himself" *(cf. Rm 5:19)*.

**Transfiguration:** The mysterious moment when, on Mount Tabor, Peter, James and John saw Jesus in glory, in the presence of Moses and Elijah *(see Mt 17:1-8)*. This was perhaps to strengthen them before the horror of Jesus' passion and death.

**Universal Church:** The Church is the universal community of believers; the People that God gathers in the whole world. She exists also in local communities (Particular Churches) and is made real as a liturgical, above all a eucharistic, assembly.

# Documents Quoted